What Reade

We are hard-wired to seek a life fully alive. To do that, we need direction toward what we are created to do. I have worked with many leaders that struggle with their self-worth, identity, and the expectations of others. One of the biggest factors I have found that holds us back from success and significance is the lack of a healthy relationship with our Dad or no relationship at all. This book is a must-read for every leader to heal themselves or equip them to heal the leaders they are sowing into. Thank you, Rick, for this incredible book on the true Father's love and how to move into the fullness of who we are!

> — **John Ramstead,** CEO Beyond Influence, Inc.
> Founder of the Eternal Leadership Podcast
> named a must for CEO's Entrepreneurs and
> Leaders by Blogspot

I grew up in a home virtually absent of a father. From him being a workaholic, to my parent's divorce, and him going to jail...he was rarely a place for me to find love, direction, and acceptance. As a new father myself, this book brought to life a deeper conviction to give my son the relationship and love both myself and Rick never received. It gives a deep and honest perspective into the desperate need we have for a father in our lives.

> — **David Shay,** CEO, Active IT Solutions, Inc.

As a mature woman who grew up with an "absent" father, this book resonated with me. Not only was I immediately drawn into Rick's relationship with his grandson, his journey to resolve the hole in his/my heart was gradually filled. By the end, I felt restored and able to shine my light, knowing my Father loves me unconditionally, and that realization leaves me feeling confident and whole. My world shines brighter now.

— **Renee E Cabourne,** Founder of Money Savvy Woman, Author of *HarMoney: A Step-by-Step Guide to Your Money...Your Rules, Your Way*

Rick's amazing book is a heartfelt love letter from God to the world. Whether you have a relationship with your biological father or not, Rick's true story of his journey from abandonment to his understanding that God is our Father, and that love is a decision, will touch you and impact all of your relationships. Rick's book should be required reading for all fathers.

— **Kevin Knebl, CMEC,** Int'l Speaker/Author/ Trainer/Executive Coach Co-Author of *The Social Media Sales Revolution: The New Rules for Finding Customers, Building Relationships, and Closing More Sales Through Online Networking* (McGraw-Hill)

This isn't just a novel; it's a journey. Rick takes you with him through the muck and mire, while showing glimpses of the deepest imaginable love. It isn't just a book for the fatherless, but one for anyone struggling to find or hold onto their own worth. It's easy to get lost in our busy and socially overwhelming world, but Rick's book is like a map to guide you. The love he feels for his grandson is one we all strive to reach. The love he feels from his God is one people have missed, lost, or constantly seek. And you learn, from Rick's experience, that it wasn't an easy path of awareness or acceptance. Read this. You'll find yourself.

— **Jennifer Duggins,** Founder of
Bohemian Gypsy Girl, LLC
Author of *Facing Giants* and other works

This book has the immediate potential for a life-changing dynamic! Fatherlessness is on the increase in our society and is a silent killer, devastating lives and relationships. *If Only I Had a Dad* is a balm for healing a society and culture which is on the decline because it's missing this essential life ingredient. This book is a blockbuster with gut-wrenching, captivating details that lay out the ultimate solution for us. Well done, Rick!

— **Rick Dempsey,** Former Pastor and
Founder of Hard Knocks Academy (formally Turning
Point School of Applied Ministry) and
Author of *Up From the Pit* and *Rush to Judgment*

Rick's story will start any reader down a path of healing, especially those who are fatherless, by helping them expose the lies in the mind and allowing them to see the truth. We have a fatherless world and so much pain stems from that problem. My prayer is that this book will add momentum to the movement rallying to help solve this problem. This book is well-written and captured my attention right from the start. Well done, Rick! Thank you for your openness and transparency to help others find what you have found, even in the pain.

— **Ford Taylor,** Founder FSH Group/
Transformational Leadership
Co-Author, *The Hike: The Missing Link to
Transformational Leadership*

An amazing journey of redemption and restoration! Rick's story gives hope to everyone who longs for a relationship they have lost or who wants to see their future ones rewritten for the better!

— **Marlia Cochran,** Speaker and Author of
*Where's My White Picket Fence?:
When A Good Girl Doubts God*

As a mother whose son gave me my first glance at real unconditional love, I fell in love with Rick's relationship with his grandson and the story of Divine Healing that it was so obviously designed to facilitate. As a daughter whose father experienced the same wounds Rick bore, my understanding and compassion dropped from my head to my heart because of Rick's willingness to show the reader all of his insides. As a seeker and messenger with a similar mission to witness the empowerment of the wounded, I am grateful to see this leader rising.

— **Amanda Johnson,** Founder of True to Intention,
Author of *Upside-Down Mommy*

A powerful example of the desperation for identity that a fatherless child can experience. Written by a grandfather who was fatherless, for his fatherless grandson, Rick poignantly captures the awe that comes with the birth of his grandson, Jaden, and his commitment to ensuring that Jaden has the father-figure he needs to find his way. A must-read for every man, fatherless or not, who must set an example for the next generation.

— **Pat Haddock,** Author of *Dear Aunt Peggy,
Emails from Petey Pup,* and *Amelia's Gift*

Rick's story is heartfelt and heart-wrenching, and I could relate to having a dysfunctional family. He wanted his dad's love and presence, and to be accepted; but instead, he went through life feeling something was missing — such emptiness. Because of his spiritual heart, God guided him so many times because he believed in Him with his whole heart. Rick's deep love for his grandson is amazing and touched my heart. Because he doesn't want his grandson to feel the way he felt during the course of his life, not having a dad, he shows him all the time how much he loves him. Rick's poetry is very lovely. You will enjoy such exquisite words.

— **Martha Perez,** Author of *Broken Pieces* and *Broken Heart*

As someone who in not an avid reader, I could not put this book down. I found myself laughing and crying and wanting to hug and salute Rick for the courage it took to live a painful story and now share it. This book is a powerfully vivid and reflective journey, inviting the senses and emotions of the reader. It encapsulates suffering in its rawest form, giving insight into an intense personal and painful reality of hurt, misunderstanding, hope, and healing.

— **Dr. Sandy Ingle, PhD,** Clinical Psychologist and Counselor

IF ONLY I HAD A DAD

FINDING FREEDOM FROM FATHERLESSNESS

BY
RICK AMITIN

If Only I Had A Dad
Finding Freedom From Fatherlessness

Published by
Rick Amitin
San Francisco, California

www.IfOnlyIHadADad.com

Copyright © 2016 Rick Amitin

Cover Design by Dan Mulhern Design
Interior Design by Dawn Teagarden
Back Cover Headshot by Gary Bowers

ISBN-13:978-1541308800
ISBN-10:1541308808

Printed in the United States of America

www.IfOnlyIHadADad.com

To Jaden, my papa boy, and inspiration!

*The picture of you taken so long ago in Muir Woods
took my breath away the moment I saw it.*

*It is such a powerful visual of the way
I felt when I was your age.*

*May my scars warn you,
My words guide you,
And my love sustain you!*

Acknowledgments

I wrote this book first to understand my own healing. Secondly, to offer a path for my grandson to follow. And thirdly, to give away what is not mine to keep.

To Divine Unconditional Love that guided me, and worked generously and patiently, to show me I am never alone and that there is forever a Place for ME!

To My Family...

To my wife, Tina. Thank you for being the one who stayed. And, for not sending me away. Your remarkable love changed the way I see the world. Your belief in me changed the way I see myself. Your strength held my brokenness until I could mend while you mended your own heart. Your support allowed me to rise from the ashes. Your courage challenged me to face my fears and live. I could not be more thankful to have you as my wife, lover, and friend. I love you!

To my children, Shannon and Monica, it is not possible to love you more than I do. I have been able to grow as a man and father as you have moved through the stages of your own lives. I had to dig deep, sometimes, to know what I was supposed to do and think and feel during many parts of our journey. I didn't always know what was right, but I always had the love to figure it out. I will never give up trying to be the father you need. I only want the best for you. I cherish your love. Being your father is an honor. I still get excited when you call me Dad.

To my daughter, Michelle. We didn't meet until you were fifteen. But from the minute I saw you, my heart was arrested. As deeply as I have ever wanted anything, I want you to know the extent of my love for you. You are a gift and everything about me includes you!

To my son-in-law, Joe. The goodness in you causes me to pause and be thankful.

To my wonderful granddaughters, Ashley, Shiela, Ali, and Shanna. You gave me my first feelings of being a grandfather. I get a little giddy when I think of you. I hold a special place in my heart for each you. And to Colby and Gary, my great grandsons, whom I've yet to meet, I can't wait to see you.

To my niece, Kimi, and my nephew, DJ, who I love as my own kids, you're the best. My heart is full of affection for you.

To Grandma, for all the love you gave me. It has lasted a lifetime!

To my sister, April, and my brother, Bobby, may my story help you find any healing you might need.

To Mother, you were there the day I was born and you were there when forgiveness birthed me again. I love you. I miss you. I will always be thankful you were my mother.

To Father, the deep sorrow will always be with me, but my sadness is forever gone!

To All of My Past and Present Friends and Mentors...

To Rick and Tami Dempsey, you have been light on many dark days, and were present for so many celebrations. Being a friend to you is a privilege I hold affectionately. Your friendship to me is nothing less than endearing. I could not have written this book without you. Your love for me, belief in me, and support of me is amazing!

To all the wonderful friendships I have now, and those that have passed through my life, thank you for sharing even the tiniest pieces of your life with me. I have a treasure box filled with sweet memories of kind, generous, and loving people. I look forward to many more great times.

To all who have nurtured my spirit, shaped my thinking, broadened my understanding, and offered insight to finding the path to authenticity, I am eternally indebted.

To the writers and creators of books, seminars, training courses, and programs from honest places that offer solutions to real life situations, I have the highest respect for you. For ministers, coaches, and mentors who look beyond present obstacles and see what can be, who invest their time, talents, and even finances to bring life to others, you make the world a better place.

To My Team...

To Amanda Johnson, you listened to me talk, visualized my story, and experienced my passion. You held the skeleton of this project in your hands and brought flesh to my message. This is the work you do, your gift, and your place of contribution. I am the recipient of your graciousness. Your ability to see power on the other side of pain is astounding. You labored to show me my own courage. For being love, and my book coach, and pulling me to the finish line, thank you.

To the True to Intention Team...

To Kathy Sparrow and the other editors, thank you for sharing your talents to add power and polish to what I put on paper.

To Dan Mulhern, thank you for taking my idea and capturing its beauty and light.

To Dawn Teagarden, thank you for making the interior of this a powerful visual journey.

With All My Love and Gratitude,
Rick Amitin

Contents

Prologue

Will the Pain Ever Stop?

Through dim glass, I faced everyday. Looking through a peep hole that only allowed me to see what was directly in front of me and inches away. My mind's eye caught glimpses of distant horizons, offering the possibility of peace and stillness. Then I returned to clenched eyes to deal with my silent agony. Like an incurable disease, the excruciating discomfort followed me wherever I went.

Will the pain ever stop?

I searched and searched. Good places and bad. Where is the antidote? The remedy? The proverbial WHY tearing at my insides. Traversing ups and downs. Forward progress disentigrating in backward spirals. I filled cracks with positive thoughts and affirming words and watched as life slipped through my fingers.

Convinced and unconvinced in the same breath.

I've got it. I've really got it this time.

No, I really didn't have it.

Do this. It will work. I guarantee it.

Another failed proclamation.

Stinging inner dialogue tainting any perception of hope.

This doesn't fit. I don't belong here. I want what I know is there, but I can't find it.

I let go of what wasn't working, but my hands couldn't release. When my heart said, "Move on," my fear tightened its grip. I deserved better, but I gave myself even worse. I was consumed with wandering as wonder beckoned my name.

How do I escape this wide-awake nightmare?

The cause is the cure.

I pierced the veil.

The pain stopped!

Introduction

I Started Without a Dad, and So Will He

"I'm ready for bed, Dad. Can you help me up?" she asked, smiling in my direction.

"Sure, Baby." I extended my arm for her to grab.

Her due date was quickly approaching and we knew she could deliver the baby anytime now. As she waddled down the hall, I sat back down, alone with my thoughts. Feeling excitement and distress, I envisioned the difference I could make.

I started without a dad and so will he.

I opened the bottle of sparkling water, poured some into my glass, and listened to it fizz. Leaning back in my seat, I began to imagine the boy that was about to join our family. What swelled up inside of me was nothing short of fierce personal resolve to protect his innocence. With the plight of the fatherless looming to wreak havoc on an unsuspecting child, my jaw tightened and my thoughts became singular.

I will counteract the elements and beat back the intangible stranglehold that sees him as easy prey. With wild abandon, I hurled my inhibitions to the four winds.

Moved by the scenes replaying themselves out in my memory, I stood up. Tears streaming down my face, I clenched my fist and stared into the abyss. I whispered for all of creation to hear: "My grand boy will know what it means to live."

My beginning was no coronation. Instead, I was crowned with the hollowness of dysfunction. My birth came with innocence that seemed to have evaporated before I left the hospital. Being wanted was a feeling I wouldn't know much about, and that emptiness would grow with me.

I have wondered, from as far back as I can remember, what my life might have been like *if only* I had received a more celebratory welcome…*if only* I had a dad.

I met my father only once. I had three stepfathers by the time I was nine. The loss of affirmation, the deep sense of unworthiness, and not knowing who I am resulted in what I describe as *Identity Theft*. The struggle to know where I belonged permeated every aspect of my life. My vulnerability led me to some traumatic life events...with some messy consequences.

My missing father unwittingly resulted in a missing God. I searched and searched for my father and, without a valid definition of masculinity, nearly any charismatic man was a candidate to feed my father hunger and fill the void inside me. I was indoctrinated with a religion that shamed me and filled me with fear, yet conformity did not heal me.

I began to filter every experience through this acquired notion of being "less than." My natural talents and gifting only served as an inauthentic introduction to a manufactured, synthetic life. Approval addiction became my pain reliever of choice, so I gravitated toward whatever and whomever made me feel desirable.

My insatiable drive to belong and communicate sent me down a path of ministry, pursuing an outlined image I could never fully capture. The more desperate I became to belong and find acceptance, the more my emptiness grew.

The plight of the fatherless had me in its clutches.

Collapsing in personal failure, I finally discovered what is real and what is not. I found the courage to go beyond the boundaries of established doctrine, surrender my excuses, overturn life-long lies, rewrite the false stories I'd created in order to find my place in the world, and live a life I no longer wish to escape.

Learning about the undeniable effects of family dysfunction, hereditary dynamics, and cultural adherence, I determined to break the cycle of destructive patterns.

Stepping away from familiar rhetoric, popular platforms, and a misinterpreted identity, I moved into the unknown — *the safest place I had ever been.* As divine intention unfolded, disillusionment ceased to dim my vision and clarity resounded, altering the lyrical inner chatter that had terrorized any hope for peace for more than fifty years.

I had been blinded by the lights of lies, perceived separation, and a sense of unworthiness dancing between me and the Light I was seeking.

As I acquired answers to my life's mysteries, and understood my fatherlessness — or more specifically, my father hunger — to be the driving force behind my behavior and thought processes, my life shifted. The salvation I expounded on as a preacher would mature into addressing father hunger as the worldwide pandemic that it is.

The great restoration ahead will be among the sons and daughters willfully neglected, violated, or outright abandoned by their fathers.

My grandson was soon to be born and the plight of the fatherless threatened his life. The closer his birth approached, the more transfixed I became. I needed the magic bullet to deal with the blight that had thwarted my purpose and would unleash destiny for him. I found the answer.

My best contribution is to share my story, with the ugly left in. If we feel special because of our details, we aren't likely to change. We can choose to hold onto our stories. Unless we want the life we don't have more than the life we do have, we will probably continue down the path we're on. But if you know, deep inside, there is more to life than what you have, this book is for you.

I doubt there is an identical twin to my experiences. At least, I hope not. Mine are loaded with pain and self-destructive patterns, and a deeply conflicting faith. However, I have found common traits among the fatherless, and some of the factors that go into determining the way one might respond to a missing or broken father. *What* we do is not as important as *why* we do it. When we learn the *why* of how we think, act, and develop habits, we are empowered to free ourselves.

Keep your note pad and/or journal handy. Better yet, download this book's companion workbook (www.IfOnlyIHadaDad.com), which includes some questions that will support you as you read this book and offer you opportunities to work through your own healing journey. As you find yourself in my story, pay attention to feelings that surface as you remember the defining moments in your life. Write down your own details and feelings, observe how I found resolution, discover your own truth, and be set free.

As you witness the powerful relationship between my grandson and me, notice how it makes your heart ache and your insides jittery. If you've never been loved by a human father-figure, and you haven't experienced the deep love that God has for you, you may find it challenging to believe that it's possible for so much love and divine intention to flow between two souls.

If your father was never there, or your father was present but unavailable, my intention is that by the last page, you'll realize that regardless of the level of abandonment and pain you have experienced, YOU HAVE ALWAYS BEEN WORTHY OF LOVE.

You deserve a rich, rewarding, and abundant life. And you can still have it.

My desire is for you to see that we are born with inherent value. We are prepackaged with purpose. We are preloaded with the necessary gifts to fulfill our destiny. But if our parents and caregivers are not prepared for the responsibility of shaping our wings, wisdom, and wonder, things can go horribly wrong… and they can also be made right again.

I'm devoted to bringing healing and hope to all who are suffering with the pain of fatherlessness and want to move forward in their lives.

Wanted

You will never taste
Bitter abandonment,
For I will not waste,
Not for a minute,
The opportunity to establish
Love's deep sentiment.

I see you.
I feel you.
I understand you.
I know you.

Not one day
Should you ever doubt
That I'm in, all the way,
For your wisdom and wings to sprout.

Before you arrived,
I wanted you.
Now that you're here,
Even more, I want you.

The gift of you
Has proven to me
That you will fully be
When yourself you clearly see.

And you must of certainty know
This is no superficial show,
For I would be haunted
If I thought you didn't know
You are wanted.

Chapter 1

I Want You!

Anticipation was so thick in the room that, if measured in smoke, it would have set off fire alarms for a thousand miles. Our daughter, Monica, was about to give birth to our grandson, Jaden Richard (named Richard after his papa). For nine months, I contemplated his arrival. And here we were, in this small intimate and bland delivery room, where the most magnificent event in the world was about to take place. My insides were swirling in a dance of cautious jubilation.

Monica was in deep labor pains. As I looked into her precious green eyes, there was the usual fear, discomfort, and expectation of every mother-to-be. My wife, Tina, was on one side of the bed; and I was on the other. Tina was in full coaching mode. She leaned in and brushed back the beautiful red hair that was sticking to the perspiration-drenched forehead of our daughter. Tina's tranquil face was now laced with concern for Monica and our soon-to-be grandson. Tears were flowing from all three of us. I was helpless to ease my daughter's pain. My fatherly instincts to protect were of no use.

Tina was more focused than anyone else in the room. She was there to see her daughter through childbirth and to welcome her grandson. The two nurses brought with them warm smiles and reassurance. One nurse was battle-tested and calm and the other was eager to learn. The young doctor, however, was a little more intense or perhaps diligent. The generic hospital curtain irritated me. It just seemed to be in the way and everyone was working around it. You could hear the hospital machines and medical staff in full motion as they all moved about in their respective areas. But anything that didn't pertain to our mission at hand seemed remote. That unique smell to every clinical setting permeated the air. The unexciting hospital wall color, sterile as it was, seemed out of place for such a huge event.

I was teary-eyed for my daughter who was in distress. But my tears were also mixed with anxious expectancy for the entrance of my grand boy. I needed to be a calm presence in the room, but I had more adrenaline than blood pumping in my body. I was in the room with Tina for the birth of both of our children. But this was somehow more eerie and majestic at the same time. I was a different man — older, wiser, with more to offer — my greying hair proof of my qualifying credentials. As a young father, I wasn't capable of the same deliberateness that I now had as grandfather.

I perceive what this boy needs from me. And I'm willing and eager to provide for him.

Jaden's father was not in the room. In fact, he decided to not be in Jaden's life. Now Jaden will deal with *the plight of the fatherless*. I was aware that all the love and attention that we will provide him will not alleviate the thoughts and feelings associated with not having a dad. My own experience provided this insight.

He will have good questions where there are no good answers.

When Jaden parted the atmosphere of this world, I had a moment like no other in the totality of my life. I became more aware than I had ever been. Significance was no longer attainable; it just was.

The nurse took Jaden to the other end of the room. I left my wife and medical staff to attend to the needs of our daughter, and I followed my boy. As she prepared him, I was right there, hovering, watching every move she made. I wanted to see any flinch of a muscle and hear any sound that might come from his mouth. I was on a mission to give my grand boy a red carpet reception. Perceiving the creative energy of life, I was standing still but pacing on the inside, waiting for the moment I could introduce Jaden to my love and affection.

After she prepared him, the nurse wrapped him in a nice, warm, baby-blue blanket; and because they were still dealing with our daughter, she handed him to me.

Divine design? I received this living, breathing gift and held him close. As the rush of love meshed the two of us as one, I reflected on what I knew about my own birth.

I arrived a little beaten up by my exit from the birth canal. Besides my unwanted entry wounds, I emerged with red hair, eyebrows that were barely distinguishable, and very light skin. Wrapped in a nice, new baby-blue blanket, I was presented to my mother.

"That's not my son!" she exclaimed. "My son has dark hair and olive skin. You need to go get *my* son!"

I don't recall this taking place. And I don't know why I was told this happened. However, neuroscience would suggest that I just might have formed a memory of the goings-on that day, based solely on the feeling in the room. Point of origin doesn't really matter. This feeling was in my mother, and I would have multiple examples to refer to in the coming years. I was not what my mother wanted, and her disappointment left an indelible birthmark.

My father was not in the room that day either. He was in prison at the time.

I was about five years old when I met my father. I was living at my grandmother's house when I was told my mother was bringing my father to meet me. Our house had two bedrooms, a small living room, a kitchen, and one bathroom with a wall that separated the bathtub from the sink and commode. We had a small, open back porch and a covered screened-in front porch. There were seven of us living there at the time.

I got cleaned up and put on my best clothes. I don't remember my ensemble; but it was, in all probability, a shirt and pair of pants from the local resale shop. I brushed my teeth without anyone telling me to. I even combed my own hair.

Anxiously, I waited, looking out of the window, asking over and over, "When are they going to get here?" I finally saw it. The old, beat-up car my mother drove pulled up in front. I jumped up and down. I don't know why, but I ran to the kitchen at the other end of the house and hid behind the counter. I think I just didn't know what to do. I heard the front door open. I heard Grandma's footsteps as she walked across the enclosed front porch. Then I heard the familiar sound of our squeaky screen door as it opened. My ears must have been in bionic mode because the din of voices and people shuffling around all sounded amplified.

I heard my father's voice for the first time as he greeted the others. I was telling myself to capture his sound. I kept thinking, *don't forget the sound of his voice.* I never wanted to be without this sound again. Then the *magic* happened. He asked, "Where's my son?"

This was a spectacular day—a day like I had never had before!

I had suffered in silence waiting to be called "son" by my father. I took notice, as kids played with their dads. I could see they were having a different life experience than I was having. There were countless times I sat alone in observation, filled with sadness because I had no dad. I didn't know it at the time, and no one else seemed to know it either, but I was grieving. And my grief was beyond my toddler skillset.

But my time had come! I couldn't wait any longer. I came running out from behind that old fifties style counter yelling, "Here I am!" And I jumped into my father's arms.

He seemed so tall and strong as we hugged each other tightly. He had the olive-colored skin my mother was so fond of. And although he had reddish-colored hair, it seemed darker because of his hair dressing. And he smelled good.

He said, "Hi, Ricky. I'm your father."

I said, "I know."

How could I not know? I had looked for my dad in the face of every man I had ever met. I didn't have a grandfather either. There was no man committed to me. There was no assurance or sense of protection. My relief at being held by my own father was a feeling that had been missing since I had been alive on the planet. For the first time in my life, I was basking in what I had witnessed only in the faces of other children.

Oh how my life changed in an instant!

I just kept looking at his smooth and handsome face, staring into his deep, dark eyes. I think I came out of the oven being detail-oriented. So, I did everything I could to take in his features. I wanted to know every characteristic and attribute that made up this man that was my dad.

For the next couple of hours, I sat on his lap at our metal kitchen table. We played games and arm-wrestled. We hugged and we laughed. I'm sure my excitement leaked out of my pores. He seemed as genuinely happy to see me as I was to see him. *How long will this last? Will I get to do this every day?* I didn't want the moment to end, not ever.

I don't know what my concepts of heaven and hell were at that age; but for those invaluable minutes, *my hell* vanished and *heaven* was all around me.

He took my tender face in his strong hands, looked me in my wide-open green eyes, and asked, "Rick, how would you like it if I was here all the time? We can go fishing, and we can play ball together. Would you like that?"

You can just imagine the emphatic five-year-old "Yes" I used to respond to his questions. His words of promise were tattooed onto my spirit.

We embraced with bona fide father-son affection. He said, "I love you, Son."

I said, "I love you, Dad."

We said our goodbyes. He and my mom walked across that same front porch and took the few steps over the short sidewalk toward the car. The air was crisp and clean and the stars appeared more illuminated than I had ever noticed. I stayed in the doorway until my grandmother made me come inside. But I stood looking out of the window as my mom and dad drove away. My heart was beating fast. I was fighting back tears.

I looked out the window for days and weeks, waiting for my father to come back. Every time the phone rang, I rushed to see if it was my dad, saying he was on his way over. The sound of every car door had me looking up to see if it was my dad. The weeks turned into months. I went from looking for my father out of the window of the house to looking for my father out of the window of my soul.

His broken promises broke me.

Why did this happen? What did I do to cause him to not come back? Did I do something wrong? Did he not want me?

"I'm not wanted" became a theme that played solo and in concert, but never ceased to play. It was like a continuous soundtrack to my life. The lack of answers left me to fill in the blanks with frustrated guesswork. I was added to the ocean of anger.

I'm not enough. I'm not lovable. I'm not worthy of being loved.

I wanted to hear my father say the normal everyday things like: "Way to go! Good job, Son! I'm so proud of you." I wanted to laugh with him at breakfast and feel safe when he tucked me into bed at night. I wanted the feeling of normality.

I wanted to be able to say, to the other kids, "This is my dad." I wanted to sit on his lap, hold his hand, and hug his neck. *I wanted my dad...and I wanted him to want me.*

Standing in the delivery room, holding Jaden in my arms and looking into his face, I used every word I knew to bless him every way I could. I knew I would never have this moment again. As tears flowed down my face, I spoke to Jaden, my papa boy:

"I love you, don't ever doubt it. I want you, and you can count on it. I have never received a more precious gift and I cherish you. There is a great man inside you, and the world will be glad you are in it. I will give you everything I have to give. I will take you fishing and we will play ball together. Thank you for coming into my life."

A nurse, having overheard my words to Jaden, stepped in close and with her own teary eyes said, "I have never heard anything like that before. This boy is blessed!"

I was vaguely conscious of all that was going on around us. But I was focused, with laser-like precision, on ensuring that the first minutes of Jaden's life were filled with love so strong that it would penetrate his skin and saturate his heart. I had to be certain he felt wanted. My inner cry begged to articulate to this priceless baby, the esteemed place he would always have with me.

After telling Jaden how much I loved him and how excited I was to meet him, I handed him off to his eager and drained mother. That first look, of a loving mother to a precious son, burned an eternal image on the landscape of my mind. I looked on with pure delight, continuing to absorb his essence. I persisted with silent prayers, staking claims that Jaden would never spend one day wondering where he belonged.

Standing next to the hospital bed, I watched as his mother and grandmother showered him with affection. I was fascinated with Jaden. I could only describe his birth as awe-inspiring. My life of *"if only I had a dad"* was dismissed as I purposed to protect Jaden from the brutal pain of abandonment. I would be one man that he could count on, always.

The first night we brought Jaden home from the hospital was extraordinary. The baby sounds, the smells, and the adults scurrying all around to meet his every need is the kind of joy that only comes from the celebration of a newborn baby. As it got late, my daughter was still quite tired and needed to sleep, but Jaden was wide-awake.

I was still up, so Monica brought him out to the living room and asked if I could take him for a while. I said, "Of course," but I was thinking, *Are you kidding me?*

The opportunity to spend quality time with my grandson excited me. Monica moved her weary body toward where I was sitting, and I received my sweet buddy. As the tired new momma retreated toward the bedroom, I stared into the soft face of my grand boy and embraced his innocence.

I sat in my rocker recliner with Jaden way into the night. I rocked him, changed him, made up songs and sang to him. I gently bounced him on my knee and rested him on my shoulder. I had a heart-to-heart talk with Jaden that lasted for hours. I said, "Jaden, I am so proud of you. You will never have to be any more than you are right now to secure your place at the table of my heart. You are a fine grandson; and I will not only celebrate your accomplishments, I will celebrate you!"

While my wife and daughter slept in their bedrooms, there was a party for two happening in the living room. I found the meaning of Heaven on Earth that night. It is a fatherless son, sitting on his fatherless papa's lap, knowing he is loved and wanted.

You Are Worthy

It won't be easy, to walk through the haze.
Life is nothing if not a complex maze,
Filled with self-inflated stealers of joy,
Thinking of their own importance, seeing you as a toy.

Don't look for others to give, what they are without.
The disappointment alone, will leave you to pout.
Here is the fact: you are not what they say.
Make your own proclamation; it's the only way.

Many life-events will place you in dismay.
Be true to yourself and don't give sway.
Know that you are equal, with any other man.
In that assurance, you can firmly stand.

Navigate with wisdom the many twists and turns.
You have a divine path with bridges to burn.
Always stay straight when you are climbing up.
Never think of yourself as a defeated pup.

There's forever a solution to complicated tasks.
Be the one who searches, not fearing questions to ask.
Don't be sold by the loud and the bold.
The riddles you solve is your pot of gold.

Before your first breath, you were assigned a place.
To live like you don't belong is the only disgrace.
Be aware of the urgency, but don't get in a hurry.
Your life will flow together when
you know you are worthy.

Chapter 2

You Are Worthy!

As all normal babies do, Jaden grew and grew. He began to discover and interact with the physical world. So many first-time experiences. His creative ways of communicating made me marvel. Such aliveness emanated from his eyes. The genius of innocence flowed free in his pursuits. So unrestricted in being here. He passed Life Participation with flying colors. He spoke volumes without the use of words.

Jaden mastered the art of mobility. First by learning to sit upright without rolling over. And then to stand, by being supported with anything he could grab to brace himself. Next came crawling, where he ventured to forbidden places with no inhibitions. He progressed to the wobble walk, where he displayed his shaky three-step moves, followed by impolite plops on his bottom.

Not one to be encumbered with discouragement, he pressed on until he was fluent in walking.

As I watched him engage with the people around him, I couldn't help but think: *The boy is a relationship guru without prior experience. He can work a room like no one else can. Without any forethought, he has people eating out of the palm of his hand. With a little gurgle or a simple grunt, he has his mother, grandmother, great grandmother, and papa competing to be the one to meet his need. He has his own castle of affection where the only people that touch him are people that love him.*

He cherished being held, coddled, and fussed over. Separating the subjects of his empire into categories, he knew just which one of us to call on to get what he wanted. Each of us was willing to accept a supporting role to this emerging star. Three women and a man, committed to meeting his every need, giving Jaden a secure beginning to his life.

He expressed independence early. Sporting only a diaper, showing his plump thighs that made us all giggle, he came into the living room carrying a gallon of milk that weighed about as much as he did. With articulate eyes and a wide *"Do you understand what I want?"* smile, he plopped the container on the ottoman. Through my laughter, I managed to pour him a bottle.

With each passing day, I witnessed Jaden unfolding with natural splendor. When his arms would reach for me to pick him up, I would melt. When he laid his head on my shoulder and threw his arms around my neck, his actions clarified the meaning of life for me.

His unsolicited kisses and hugs made me want to make time stand still.

Right now, he is living without fear. He has everything he needs for the moment. But how long do we have before his missing father becomes an issue?

I was desperate to lessen the impact of fatherlessness in his life. With steel determination and a fluid heart, I pondered a number of possibilities.

Would Jaden ever know his father? Would a stepfather move onto the landscape of his life?

I knew what a missing father did to me. Being hungry for masculine attention can make one vulnerable. I had three stepfathers by the time I was nine, and I would have been better off with none. Knowing I couldn't control all the variables in his life, I purposed to be a grandfather that worked to straighten the bend in his sacred path, and help him steer clear of some of the painful, fatherless trails I was forced to take.

It was a beautiful summer day. I heard birds chirping in the dawn of morning. The sun was now center sky and shining bright. There was a gentle breeze rustling the trees into a magical background of angelic harmony. People were outside, sitting on their porches, watching the neighborhood kids playing and laughing. The sound of water sprinklers was prevalent, as we raced back and forth, cooling ourselves with drops of homemade rain.

It could have been a very good day in my nine-year-old life, except that my mom was missing.

Being a single mother of three, my mom had us babysat by nearly anyone she could find. This time, her sister was looking after us. I loved my Aunt Jo. She was always pleasant, patient, and loving. My mom should have returned home after her eight-hour shift; but it was the middle of the next day, and we hadn't heard a word from her. I could see the concern in my aunt's eyes. She called the truck stop where my mom waitressed to inquire if she was somehow still there. She was told that my mom left with a truck driver but that we shouldn't worry...she would be back soon.

Looking toward the street every few minutes, I wondered, *What if something is wrong? What if she never comes back? What will happen to us? Who will care for us?*

It was two difficult weeks before Mom came home.

I was outside playing when I noticed her car coming down our road. Without remembering how upset I was, the instant excitement of seeing her had me running toward her. As I got close enough to see into the car, I stopped dead in my tracks. Mom was not alone — there was a man with her.

Mom had been married three times, and I had already lived through a number of her boyfriends. To say the first several years of my life were filled with turmoil would be putting it mildly. It was common for me to be apart from my mom and siblings, and it seemed like every time a new man entered the picture, bad things happened.

Who is this guy? What trouble will he bring with him? Experience had me bracing for the worst.

Hot and sweaty from playing in the summer heat, I stood numb as Mom drove by toward our house. The beautiful day faded from my awareness. My emotions formed a perfect storm. In slow motion, I stepped from the patch of grass I was standing on and moved down our dirt and gravel road. I took my time as I walk toward home. I watched as they got out of the car and went into the house. I arrived home, but didn't go inside. I didn't want another rejection. I didn't want another experience of my mother choosing a man over me.

Where is my father? Why doesn't he come and save me?

This was a common day, but I just didn't believe this was how it was supposed to be. I couldn't explain what was wrong, but I could feel it.

Why isn't my mom happy with me and my sister and brother? We can be a family. We don't need a strange man.

I could hear my mom and her sister arguing as I approached the house, and it was getting louder. My aunt had every right to be upset. She had not only been taken advantage of, she was also subjected to many days of worry. I walked up the three steps of our porch, took two steps to reach the doorway, and stood there peering into the conflict. Through the screen door, I could see my aunt was standing across the room near the kitchen sink, arms folded. My mom was sitting at the dining table with her legs drawn up to her chest, smoking a cigarette. She saw me standing there, and our eyes met, but neither of us spoke.

I observed the man who was also sitting at the dining table with his back to the door. His short-sleeve shirt had the sleeves rolled up, exposing larger than normal muscles. He had a full head of black hair. I despised him without delay. I couldn't see his face, nor did I want to.

He must be the reason we are all going through this!

After a few minutes, my mom finally spoke to me, "Come inside and go into the living room with your brother and sister." I paid attention to the strange feelings I had as I walked past the man. He turned and looked at me, offering a smile. I gave him only a purposeful gaze in return.

I moved across the black and white kitchen linoleum flooring as fast as I could. It was only a few steps but seemed to take forever. As I stepped into the living room, I saw fear in the faces of my brother and sister. I joined them on the melancholy-drenched couch. This wasn't the happy reunion I had imagined.

Mom followed me into the room, her face still flush from arguing with her sister. The look in her eyes scared me. She threw herself into the chair, and I intuitively braced myself for what was coming next.

With a tightly stressed lip, stern penetrating eyes, and a pointed finger that presented itself like a weapon, my mom began to speak to us with words sharper than a strapped razor: "I love this man and he is going to live with us," and, "If you do anything to chase him off, I will kill you!"

My seven-year-old sister cried out loud. My four-year-old brother leaned back and curled up as if to withdraw inside himself. My nine-year-old experience was different.

My body tensed up in anger. My fists clenched and my jaw tightened. *Again? Really, Mom? You are going to do this again?* My next impulse was to provide safety for my siblings. *How can I stop this?* I resisted the urge to go into the kitchen and throw the man out. But I knew I wasn't big enough. I knew I couldn't save any of us!

Why isn't my dad here to protect me? He said he was going to come. He said he would be here all the time. Where is he?

I was still looking for him. I knew he was coming. I just knew it.

If only I had a dad...!!! If only...? If only...?? If only...???

There was a deafening pause to my mother's diatribe, broken only by the tears and sobs coming from my frightened siblings. I had tears too, but they were tears of deep forming resentment. My mom asked if we understood, but got up and walked out before I could respond. I knelt on the throw rug in front of my brother and sister. I took them both into my arms, and I told them everything was going to be alright. But I didn't know if that was true.

I slipped into a back bedroom where it was dark and silent so that I could be alone. The voice in my head began to speak:

You're worthless, Rick!
You're not important!
You don't matter!
Your mom doesn't love you!

You're not what she wants!

You're in the way!

Is this normal? Am I defective somehow? Doesn't my mom understand how much I love her? Something must be wrong with me...

I could not secure any release from the heart-breaking and devaluing rhythms that ricocheted throughout my body.

You're not good enough. You're not loved enough. You're not wanted enough. You're not enough. My mom just didn't understand how I felt.

I didn't think it was possible, but each passing day brought a deeper love for Jaden and whenever my mind wandered to the various scenarios that might affect him, there was a pause that took my breath away. As an infant and toddler, I gave him attention, played with him often, and held him close. I would gently press him into my chest and ask, "Do you feel that grand boy? Papa's heart is full of love for you."

In my mind, I adorned myself in every conceivable uniform. Whenever he would need a cheerleader or a coach or just his papa, I vowed to be ready as the fatherly presence that would observe, commemorate, and mark his life.

While Jaden began his life living in our home, I knew that would likely change.

Whether he is near or far, I must find a way to be there for him. I asked the questions: *What will it take to maintain the light in his eyes? How will we nurture his wings, wisdom, and wonder?*

One evening, I settled into our soft brown leather couch, convinced I was being tricked into watching a chick flick disguised as a family film. The smell of hot buttered popcorn and the promise of a few more snacks made the situation more palatable. Without warning, I was rallied to one of those moments in time. When Viola Davis' character spoke to her charge in *The Help*, I was inspired. Greatly inspired, I used some of her words to express some of the words to Jaden that I wished my father had shared with me.

I told him, "You are smart. You are kind. You are important. You can do anything. And your papa loves you."

I repeated this to Jaden until he was old enough to say it himself. I had these words made into a black and white sign and hung it on the wall in his room. I taught him to memorize it. Jaden is six years old as I write this, and even though he lives away from me now, I ask him to say this to me every chance I get.

And I make a big deal whenever he repeats this mantra. I make him feel like he just hit a home run or cured cancer. I have responded this way from the beginning, and I took notice of his reaction to my celebration. His big brown eyes get even bigger. And his smile increases in abundance. There is no question that he approves of my approval — and I am grateful that this was a well-established practice before he moved away.

Shortly after Jaden turned two years old, his mother decided to relocate to San Francisco. I was heartbroken. I couldn't get my mind wrapped around him not being in my life on a daily basis. I was lost and struggled to conceive a new strategy to stay connected to him.

I am thankful for video calls. There were days when just seeing his face and hearing his voice was all I needed. The first time we called on the computer and he saw me on the screen, he reached out to touch me and asked, "Papa, can I come in there?" I wished I could reach through that computer and hold him.

Jaden came back to Indiana for the summer and I was filled with joy. I could see how much we had missed in the few months he was away. Potty-training was going well. He fed himself with little assistance. He was amazing at expressing his thoughts. He even taught us how to do some things on an iPhone.

On our way to the park one day, he asked, "Papa, how come I don't have a dad in my family?"

Well, there it is. He isn't three years old yet. What did he see or hear to open him up to this realization?

I did my best to explain that families come in all shapes and sizes...trying to avoid the harsher reality. It seemed to satisfy him for the moment.

The next day he said, "Papa, when you grow up, you can be my dad!"

My heart caught in my throat, and all I could say was, "Thank you. I would love that."

I smoothed his hair as he drifted off to sleep, and wandered deeper into thoughts of how I could increase his sense of worthiness, because I've come to believe that is what makes all things possible.

In a soft, barely perceptible whisper, I began, "You're not alone, Jaden. You are complete. You are enough all by yourself, and you are able to do anything. You are wanted and you are loved. The poet Rumi said, 'Live life as if everything is rigged in your favor,' and this is my desire for you, Jaden — that you will not create a conspiracy in your mind.

"I am certain the lies of the fatherless will trouble you. I know they are floating through your mind already, forming as a lyric to play continuously in your subconscious. The denigrating tune will say things like, 'I'm not wanted' and 'I'm messy' and 'I'm bad, defective, and I don't belong.' They are all lies, Jaden. You are worthy! You must know that you are worthy!"

Never Too Messy

Life begins messy.
That's how we play the game.
You will be guilty,
But don't ever live in shame.

You start at the top
And you will fall down.
Get up, get up, and do not stop.
Own your heart and don't let it drown.

The world has arms that are open to you.
Look real close and you will see it is true.
Possess your course for all you will be.
Forgive the blind that will not see.

Learn the fallacy of how to compete.
Know the secret is what you complete.
You are more than enough, for all you will ever do.
Remember that this life, is what you pass through

Life ends messy.
That's how we play the game.
All guilt is gone,
There is no evidence of shame.

Chapter 3

I Love You,
Even When It's Messy!

When Jaden was four weeks old, his mother went back to work. Tina was working also; and I had just sold a business, so I was elected to keep Jaden on Fridays by myself. *Divine design?* Yes, I believe so.

I tried to be a hands-on dad with my children. I wanted to share special moments with them. I had no problems changing them when they were wet, but I was reduced to complete inoperability when their diapers were messy. I tried, I really did; but after throwing up, I admitted to incurable diaper incompetence.

It wasn't very long at all, maybe fifteen minutes, after Monica and Tina left for work that first day when I breathed the aroma of my grand boy and knew clearly what was required of me. I laid him down, undid his one-piece pajamas, and opened his diaper.

Dear God in heaven!

I was a firsthand witness that all corruption from the beginning of time had landed in my grand boy's diaper. It was out on both sides and ran all the way up to the back of his head. I was certain that somebody had put an already soiled diaper on him.

There is simply no way all this came from this baby.

I didn't throw up. I didn't even gag. It was on his pajamas, the changing blanket, the bedspread, my pants and shirt. And yes, it got on my fingers. It took a whole box of wipes, a bath, and a change of clothes for both of us, but we accomplished our mission. I talked to Jaden the whole time, telling him how much I loved him and how glad I was that I get to share every minute of his life. I told him how much it meant for me to have this experience with him.

I don't want him to feel that he is "too messy" to love because I know that feeling.

There was no better time to be living at Grandma's than on a Sunday morning. The smell of sweet rolls in the oven motivated me to get ready for church in a flash. When I sat down at the table and they put one of those rolls in front of me, I required no further religious training. At five years of age, I knew that God was a good God! After all, He made sweet rolls.

Sunday mornings had their element of chaos. I stood beside the car as everyone piled in. No need to rush since I always had to sit on someone's lap for the seventeen-mile trip to church, for which there was enough hairspray, perfume, and cologne in the car to take a little boy to the brink of requiring medical treatment. I didn't need God to grant me heavenly visions; by the time we got to church, I was hallucinating.

Northern Indiana could have good weather on accident. But it is not advisable to plan for it. This was an exceptional day. Warm, but not too hot, with minimal humidity. As we pulled out of the driveway, I noticed that the trees were thick with abundant and colorful green leaves. The street my grandmother lived on would not be anything special to most, consisting of modest houses and a striving class of people, but it was uniquely comforting to me because I associated it with her.

My mother was living only twenty minutes away, but I didn't see her very often. I don't remember where my siblings were at the time, but they were not living with Mom either. It was not unusual for a man to be with my mom; and each time it happened, I would wrestle with painful feelings. *Why does a stupid man get to be with my mom and I have to be away?* This was not an easy concept for a little boy to process.

We often went by her house on our way to and from church. She lived on a busy and congested road. Even though we would pass by at sixty to seventy miles an hour, I would strain to see if I could catch a glimpse of her through the car window. I never did see her during any of those trips. I usually didn't say anything, but my eyes were surely filled with sadness.

On our way home after church that day, my grandma asked me if I wanted to spend the afternoon with my mom.

"Well yeah! Can I? Can I? Can I?" I jumped up with excitement.

My mom routinely hurt and disappointed me, but I was a little boy with natural tendencies toward motherly affections. I don't know which feeling was more powerful — wanting to be with my mother or my mother wanting to be with me.

As we approached my mother's driveway, my uncle slowed the car down, but my heart sped up. My mom's house was behind a larger house that was being used as a business. We turned onto the gravel driveway, and I felt the car's reaction as it rolled over stones. I had a slight pause in the midst of my excitement.

Is she alone?

As we got to the house, we honked the horn and Mom opened the door. My mom was kind of tiny and I thought she was beautiful.

My grandma rolled down the window and said, "Rick wants to spend the afternoon with you. We will pick him up on our way back to church tonight."

My mom said, "No, I can't. Not today. I have some things I have to do."

There was an explosive reversal in my built-up enthusiasm. I heard the ever-present chatter inside:

He's not my son. I don't want him. Just go away. After their usual back and forth, where my mom stood her ground and my grandmother shamed her thoroughly, my grandma took me out of the car and force-fed me to the woman who had brought me into this world.

I heard every word of my mom's resistance. The look on her face no longer matched her initial relaxed and pleasant inclinations. She was upset, and I was not sure of what to do or say. As the car started to leave, I almost stopped them to tell them I had changed my mind. But my mom led me into the house. I was relieved when there was no one else there.

Mom's house was small but functional, although it seemed big for one person. She always kept a clean house, and she was doing some decorating. In fact, she was in the middle of hanging some things on the wall when we interrupted her.

Maybe if I'm useful, she will want me to live with her!

She had put a nail in the wall and was going to hang a decorative plate over a chair.

I grabbed the plate and said, "I'll do it, Mom."

She said, "No, I will do it."

"But, Mom, I want to help," I insisted. I wanted to gain her approval. I wanted her to want me! I stood on the chair, placed the plate on the nail, and asked, "Is this the way you want it?"

"Yes," she finally acquiesced, and I let go of the plate. It fell to the floor and broke into pieces. I couldn't breathe, waiting for her to say something. But she didn't say anything. She just stared at me.

Oh no! She will never want me. I can't do anything right. I'm too messy for her to love me.

After a few seconds, which seemed like an hour, I managed to say, "I'm sorry, Mom. I didn't mean to do it. I just wanted to help."

"You should have let me do it!" she exclaimed. "Just go sit down and let me finish what I'm doing."

I went to the small floral couch where I sat...afraid to move or speak. My mom hardly spoke to me the entire day. As I sat being mostly ignored, I tried to think of what I could do so she wouldn't be mad at me. I wanted to run back to Grandma's house.

I hate feeling unwanted! My heart hoped for my father. He would make things better.

The lyrics to my life song were taking shape in my mind.

I know we ate something, but I don't remember what it was. I tried to act like nothing was wrong as I sat alone, choking on the tension in the air. *I love my mom so much. What am I doing wrong?* I kept myself busy with the few toys, books, and puzzles she had, while she stayed in her bedroom watching television.

When I heard the car coming up the driveway, I wasted no time saying goodbye. I was at the car before it came to a stop. I just wanted to get away from the feelings I was having.

As we drove away, I was afraid of the questions I knew would be asked.

"Did you have a good time with your mom?"

"Oh yes," I said.

"What did you do?"

"We decorated and then we played games. After dinner, Mom gave me some candy. Mom loves me very much and she wants me to live with her very soon." When my imagination was on good behavior, it was my best friend.

As we drove away, I felt the nearness of distance. I didn't know what to do with my feelings. My emptiness was full. *I don't know where my father is and my mother doesn't want me!* I was overwhelmed as the deep sense of separation cut a little deeper. *Where do I belong?*

I could feel the lightheartedness in the car as they sang on the way to church, but I couldn't sing. There was no song in my heart. I wanted to scream in order to release the hurt I was feeling. Without the ability to even begin to explain my pain, I sat still, observing my thoughts and emotions—writing a story that didn't have a happy ending.

As the car sped down the road, I became less aware of my surroundings. I was altogether engaged with the producers of my soundtrack as we worked out the remaining lyrics for my continuous play album. *You have a father. You met him. He is real. He is out there somewhere. He just isn't here for you. Your mom is nice to you sometimes, but she doesn't want you. She doesn't love you. Messy, Messy, and Messy — You're too messy to Love.*

Like most songwriters, especially the ones just starting out, I didn't have any idea if I was writing a hit song. I didn't know it at the time, but this song would top *my* charts for years. Before it was over, it would go to number one and *my* whole world would dance to the tune.

We arrived at church. I didn't want to be there and stayed with grandma instead of going to children's church. I remember the message that night. It was on hell. They made it so real, I thought my leg was on fire and rubbed my pants to put it out. I was sure that I was the imperfect sinner that would spend eternity in fiery torment.

The day was sunny, hot, and humid, but Jaden wanted to hit balls. We were using a fat plastic bat and a big rubber ball. Our grass was thick, lush, and dark green. We had a couple of big trees and two sheds to navigate, but there was ample room behind the house for hitting the ball. A short fence provided just the right target for the thrill of a home run. I had demonstrated hitting the ball for Jaden. I sent a couple over the fence and explained, "That's called a homer!"

Jaden gleefully announced, "I want to hit homers." I had him line up with a home plate. I positioned his feet and showed him how to hold the bat. Then I stepped back to pitch him the ball.

Something my father never did with me.

It went well for a few minutes. He was a natural. He was coordinated. He even hit a homer. It was thrilling. I was excited to see the enthusiasm swell up inside him as he felt his achievements. I knew he was filled with joy at hitting the ball over the fence just as he had seen me do. I jumped up and down cheering him on. Then he missed a few balls and didn't make good contact on a few more.

At four years of age, he began to be silly and not try very hard. I got a little impatient and reminded him that it was hot. "If you don't want to *do it right,* I'm going in the house."

He kept up being silly and I finally said, "Okay, I'm going in." I put the ball down. "Let me know when you want to *do it right,*" I bellowed. I had used this tactic successfully, before, with other things.

As I started to walk away, Jaden dropped his bat and cried out, "You are always leaving me."

His words froze me mid-stride and made my heart stop altogether. I recognized the message my actions were conveying: You are too messy to love. The last thing I wanted him to feel. I was causing him to feel unwanted, unworthy, and too messy for my time and attention.

It was then that I knew Jaden would be shaped by the way I make him feel, not by the words I say. He would incorporate into his life the things he sees much more than the words he hears. He was learning my lyric and humming my tune. He was feeling my fatherlessness and maybe his own.

I took a deep breath to assess my next move...my next word.

If Jaden, at four years of age, can attach such meaning to my behavior, I need to be more deliberate than ever to provide a different experience for him. If he could believe that I would leave him over a ball and bat, how will he ever trust me when life really gets messy? I have to address this now.

He had run off, and I found him crouching behind the fence. I looked into his face and saw myself fifty years younger. I had caused Jaden to feel things I never wanted him to feel. I picked him up. I walked to the deck and sat down, holding him in my arms.

I told him how sorry I was that I made him feel that way. "Sometimes Papa makes mistakes, but I want you to know that I will never leave you. You don't have to do everything right for me to love you, Jaden."

He hugged me as tight as ever and said, "That's okay, Papa. I know you didn't mean it."

Who is teaching whom? I wondered to myself quietly as he got down from my lap and went off to play.

I sat there, my heart beating fast and my lungs gasping for air. I was trying to catch up to my speeding thoughts. The sun was beaming on the crown of my head. I felt the sweat drip from my chin. My tears mixed with perspiration. As I reflected on my life, I realized there was still some pain lodged in my secret places. I suddenly understood that if I wasn't careful, I could pass on to Jaden things that I detested.

I came face-to-face with my own truth. My own feelings of being *too messy to love* were there, waiting to be told what to do. I took the Vinyl LP out of my heart. The lyric that had been with me for so long had out-lived its time. I rewrote my own lyric to be able to offer Jaden my best.

As I watched him play, I vowed to him and to the broken little boy still inside of me: "You will never be too messy to love. Messy has nothing to do with it. Love never turns and walks away."

That's "My" Boy

Release the balloons, give cigars,
and place the yard sign.
It is official, it is confirmed: it is a boy this time.
I have held others and I have bought them toys,
Now it is my turn to say — that's "my" boy.

I am biased with spectacular joy.
Heaven has opened up and sent this boy.
Maybe I should be polite and not annoy,
But I can't help myself — that's "my" boy.

I held him, he crawled, and then he walked.
It was no time at all before he talked.
I showed him off to everyone, and that was my ploy.
I could not wait to say — that's "my" boy.

He's been adored, everywhere he ever went.
Love, belonging, and affirmation is his scent.
He can be bold but mostly he is coy.
I am so proud to say — that's "my" boy.

He has inner strength, and a tender heart.
It is his empathy, which sets him apart.
The whole universe is to be his employ.
I am blessed to say — that's "my" boy.

He has wings, wisdom, and wonder.
The world will marvel at how he makes thunder.
Make no mistake, he's not a decoy.
He is the real thing — and that's "my" boy.

Chapter 4

That's My Boy!

Every day, when Jaden would wake up, it was like experiencing the sun rising for the first time. It didn't matter what room I was in, I would keep the house silent to not miss his daily arrival. Before there were words, his sounds were absolute intelligence summoning me to his side. It was my invitation to witness his presentation of the divine. I would rush to his bed to take in his innocent and undisturbed presence.

At first, he would just be lying there, in his white crib, usually on his back uttering indecipherable words that I understood perfectly. He would smile, without fail, when I came into his view, and I would think, *Oh, how I am drawn to his predictable light-filled eyes. His inevitable ear-to-ear grin is more than priceless. He is a gift, a piece of God that I want to unwrap with care.*

Then one day Jaden changed my world.

The heat was still rising from my single-dripped coffee. I had just settled into the couch in our living room with the seventeen-foot cathedral ceiling that made me feel unrestricted. I had not yet taken my first sip when I heard the joyous sound of his voice.

He's up early!

I scurried to his bedside. Our eyes met as he lay waiting for me to arrive with my customary "That's my boy!" greeting. This time he reached out for me. No star athlete setting a record or concert pianist delivering his best performance could feel any more exhilaration than I felt in that moment. His short arms, fully extended, saying, *I want you.* My love was being reciprocated. Maybe he would have reached for anyone that appeared at his bedside — but on this day, for the first time, he reached for me.

Is this what God feels toward us? The thought floated through my mind and then right out as soon as I picked him up and began our day.

The normal progression ensued. I would find him sitting up and reaching for me. Then he would be standing with his little hands holding the railing and reaching for me. My greeting was the same each and every time, "That's my boy!" I don't remember a day when his glamorous smile wasn't shining back at me. This was our daily ritual, his smile and my greeting that hastened in the truest spirituality imaginable. I was becoming image-enabled, discovering the intention of fatherhood in its various designated forms.

When Jaden began to walk, I continued to keep the house silent in the mornings. If I was in the living room, I would hear his first movements and knew when his plump little feet touched the wood floor that it was only a few steps before I would see him. If I was in the office, I would hear him pitter-pat down the hall, step down into the living room, cross the room, step up to the kitchen and onto the vinyl floor (which made its own distinct sound), and then appear in the doorway.

Either way, I delivered the same performance. I would stop whatever I was doing the second I saw him and leap to my feet in a papa jig and sing, "That's my boy! That's my boy!"

And Jaden always had the same reaction. He released an uncontrollable smile. His movie star eyes increased in size and dismissed any darkness that may be lurking. He would say, "Hi, Papa," and then give me a hug.

I do this every time we are together. And when he lived far away, every time we Facetimed, the instant he came on the screen, I did the same thing.

When we were planning for Jaden to come back to Indiana and spend the summer, he said he was excited to come and that he missed being with us. His lifestyle had changed. At our house, he could easily go outside to play. He had a quad to ride, and just outside the door he could shoot his targets, have water fights, or hit balls. He could fill his bird feeders, blow bubbles, work in the garden, or sit in the hot tub. He loved to ride around on the lawn tractor. I used to hook up the wagon and pull him around in it. He treated the wagon like it was his personal chariot and sat looking like life could get no better.

Living in a fifth floor apartment, so many things he was used to doing were just not available to him. While the city life was providing a different perspective and offering him additional experiences, we could tell that he missed many of the things we offered. We decided we would try and do as many of the things he missed as we could. We asked him what he missed the most, expecting him to name some of his activities — Chuck E. Cheese, Monkey Joe's, The Bounce House, or maybe riding his quad.

Instead, he said, "What I miss the most is Papa's words when I come out in the mornings."

I smiled, thinking about the only bond I had as a child that even came close to the one I now shared with Jaden. And then my heart sank a little as I realized how much I still missed my grandma after all these years.

It was so hard to let her go.

I got out of the car and walked into the airport. I was usually excited to travel, but this day was different. Just a few days earlier, I had buried my grandmother. She was my mom's mother, but I had spent so much time with her that she felt like *mom* to me. I had never lost anyone close, and my grief was indescribable. She was only fifty-five years old when she passed, and I was nineteen.

I made my way through the crowd, found the right gate, and checked in. As I boarded the plane and located my seat, I settled in for the five-hour flight back to my duty station in California. While everyone else was boarding, shoving bags into overhead bins, seating themselves, and buckling up for takeoff, I was lost in contemplation of what my life would be like without Granny.

I yielded to sadness as the plane pushed back from the gate. I was so relieved that no one was sitting in the seats next to me. I wanted space to be alone. I knew it was final. I would never see her again. My grandmother's love had been the only love I never doubted. She told me she loved me like I was her own son, and I believed her. She often greeted me with, "There's my boy!"

Will I ever be loved like that again? Will there ever be another person that will choose to sit in my mess with me instead of abandon me or send me on my way again?

Grandma had also exposed me to things of faith. Despite all of the family breakups and dysfunction, and inconsistent spiritual development, I had many memories of experiences at church that had stuck with me. I was afraid of God mostly, believing I was in constant danger of eternal judgment. They said I had to be good to receive good things from God, and yet the feelings I had of not being good enough were also being reinforced at my church, so much so that I lived in terror whenever I made a mistake or did something wrong.

One time, when I was about twelve years old, I smoked cigarettes with some boys. That evening, I was lying in bed thinking that I had sinned when a bolt of fear shot through my body from head to toe. Drenched in sweat, I went to the phone to call Grandma. I thought God had come and taken all His people away and I got left behind. But, I knew if she answered the phone, then I was safe. She would never be left behind. My Aunt Brenda answered and I belched, "Where's Grandma?" Aunt Brenda said she was lying down with one of her migraines. "When's the last time you saw her? Can you go see if she's in the bed?" I could hear that I was really worrying my aunt, so I tried to rid my fear by asking her: "If God came to rapture the church, do you think you would go?" My aunt said she thought so, and I said, "That's not good enough. Please go make sure Grandma is still here."

Church-life was a mixed bag for me — like everything else in my life. Summer camps were a big deal at our church; but as a kid, I never got to go to any of them. Many young people were learning to play music and sing. I stood on the sidelines only wishing I could, too. A couple of highly promoted youth mission's trips took place, but they were not meant for me. When I heard the kids talk about the fun they had, I felt left out. I was told we just didn't have money for such things.

I was allowed at church, but not included. It looked a lot like my non-church life, I mused as the jet moved through the clouds. I occasionally glanced out of the window to take in the sights from thirty thousand feet.

I had a faraway awareness of people moving about the plane, but I was preoccupied thinking through my life up to this point.

There was one spiritual experience, rising above the rest, which happened when I was ten years old.

Our church was a growing dynamic Pentecostal church, where I was used to seeing people demonstrate their worship and express their emotions during services.

This Sunday morning was particularly moving. As the organ fired up and the rest of the orchestra piped in and the singers began to sing, we were all, young and old, seemingly whisked into a heavenly place. I stood quietly, observing at first, watching people begin to cry in unison. Slowly, many people were moving toward the altar at the front of the church and kneeling down and I felt my own invitation to respond. As I took my place near the altar, I was feeling something I had never felt before.

I was already well-acquainted with deep pain and had shed many tears of sorrow in my young life. But I couldn't understand what was going on inside of me. I only knew I wanted more of what I was feeling. I had my face buried in my hands and my tears of relief would not stop. I was trying not to think. I just wanted to linger in the gentle warmth.

Suddenly, there was an arm around me and a voice whispering in my ear, "Are you okay, Rick?" I recognized my pastor's voice. It was more than pitch and tone. It was his fatherliness. He was a God-like creature to me. I was a little afraid of him, but wanted very much to be near him.

That's why the words that escaped my lips shocked me, "Pastor, I think I'm called to preach." I don't know why I said it, and I had no idea how he would respond.

Without batting an eye, he looked straight at me and said, "Rick, I think you *are* called to preach. I want you to come with me."

We got up, and he led me out of the auditorium, weaving our way through the kneeling crowd, through the nursery, and through the back door to his office.

As we walked, I felt the impact of this moment. He had a church with a few hundred members, and he stepped away from all of them to talk to me.

So this is what a father is like.

The office was small, and the walls were lined with books. He took two books from the shelf and handed them to me, inviting me to read them. Then he instructed me to start reading the New Testament. He explained that I might not understand everything, but it would be good for me to read it all the way through.

"Rick, I know you have a difficult life, but God will give you a better life if you will let Him." In the tenderness of the moment, a calling was established and an identity was formed.

He prayed for me, hugged me, and then led me back into the church auditorium.

I wish he were my father. I'm going to become a minister and make him proud of me someday. Yes! I am going to be a preacher!

The announcement came over the loud speaker, "Please return to your seats and fasten your seatbelts. We will begin our descent for landing and have you on the ground in about twenty minutes."

The death of my grandma and her final words to me had cracked my heart and my calling wide open again: "I love you like you are my own son! I know GOD has plans for you. Don't run from Him."

My Uncle Jodie, an ordained minister, helped me revisit spiritual things in the days just after she passed, and made me think that God did have plans for my life. I was returning to the Marines a changed man, and determined to pursue my purpose, even though Church was still sweet and sour for me.

I had experienced love and judgment in church and I had also experienced faith and fear. I was confused as to whether I was good enough for heaven or destined for hell. My last step toward God had made me keenly aware: *Church-life can be dangerous.*

Just over a year before, I was stationed in Okinawa, Japan. I had not been involved in church in a few years, and a lady from the church I grew up in made it a point to write to the men and women serving in the military. She found out I was on active duty and sent me a letter and a cassette tape of a sermon. Ten thousand miles from home, seventeen years old, with a growing sense of unworthiness and shame, I was easily moved to emotion.

It was a Monday and I was off duty because I had worked the weekend. With the barracks empty, I listened to the sermon. Afterwards, I was lying in my bunk, thinking about the sermon and the many other sermons I had heard when I suddenly felt something pulling me down. *Toward hell?* It was so real I jumped off my bunk to look underneath expecting to see something there. I just knew a demon spirit was assigned to my destruction.

A fellow marine came in just in time to see me crouching on the floor and asked what I was doing. I told him I thought something was under my bed, but I must have had quite a look on my face, since he asked if I was okay. I said I was fine...but I wasn't.

I was afraid of hell. I was afraid of not being saved. I was more afraid that I wasn't good enough for God at all. In fear, I again looked to the heavens.

When I realized the military didn't offer my brand of church, I found two families, with my faith that were meeting together. I joined them on Sunday. One family had five children, were fun, loving, played music and sang, and laughed a lot. After some time of getting to know each other, this family somewhat adopted me.

I started spending a lot of time with them, eventually spending nights and weekends. I called them Mom and Pop, and I felt very much like the older brother who had fun with all the kids. It was great and I loved it. It felt like I was part of the family. I was young, lonely, searching for my identity, and hungry for a father. And bam, there was this great man who took me in.

I didn't know there were problems in their marriage, and I didn't know the trouble lurking behind the scenes. So when she kissed me on the lips, I was completely caught off-guard. At seventeen, maybe eighteen by then, my emotions went into orbit. It shook me up so badly, I spoke to a superior about it, who advised me to stay away and never go back.

I did, at first. But the man came looking for me. Told me it was a misunderstanding. I went back, only to have them both separately share their problems with me. There appeared to be some very deep issues between them. I left the day I received all this information, and never returned to their house again. Nothing in my life had prepared me for anything like this, but I knew that I didn't become a part of this family to cause pain and destruction. Actually, it was quite the opposite.

She left him, got an apartment, and contacted me. And a familiar lyric took over, and my deep feeling of unworthiness made the feeling of being desirable to an attractive older woman irresistible.

I moved in with her and we stayed together for a short time until she was forced to return to the States, without her kids. A few months later, I returned and met up with her. I didn't know what the plan was exactly, but I went on to visit my family. A couple of weeks later, she informed me she quit her job and was flying to Indiana to meet up with me and…she was pregnant. When my family learned I was involved with a married woman, the same age as my mother, with five kids, claiming to be pregnant with my baby — let's just say, it didn't go over very well. Some said I was looking for a mother. Some asked how I could know I was the father and not her husband. At eighteen, this was too much to deal with, and I was not capable of knowing the right thing to do; so with my family's persuasion to end it, I said goodbye to her and returned to the service.

I shook my head, as if trying to shake out those memories as I peered out of the plane and saw the beautiful San Diego Bay. The palm trees moved me. I had a true love affair with California. When I stepped outside of the airport and felt the warm air and sunshine, it was like a private greeting to welcome my return. I needed a taxi to get me to the bus station so that I could catch a bus to Camp Pendleton. As the taxi navigated the city, everything I saw had the familiarity of a lifetime. As I embraced the kind feelings of hospitable surroundings, I was also aware of my new commitment and the fact that I would have to walk through much temptation, reintroduce myself to my military buddies, and be strong.

I grabbed my bag, stepped from the bus, and began to walk toward my barracks. The base had its own feel, smell, and sound. I didn't see anyone I recognized as I travelled down the blacktop road with loose scattered stones. Every step I took had the sensation of walking in a brand new life. This was Monday, late afternoon, and I couldn't wait to go to church on Sunday.

The possibility of fulfilling my ten-year-old call to ministry had never been very far from my deepest thoughts. I didn't know what to do or how to do it. But I was convinced that my starting point was a church where I could learn, develop, and seize spirituality. My uncle had given me the address to a church that I would attend on the weekend.

Finally, after a long week of my friends scratching their heads and murmuring bewilderment, trying to figure out who was in my body, Sunday came. I rose early, put on a suit my buddies had never seen before, and sat quietly, hoping to avoid their snide remarks. I had abruptly quit smoking and drinking, didn't want to hear dirty jokes, and stopped cursing. They didn't know what to make of the new me. But, there were lots of comments. When it was time to go, I grabbed my bible and headed to church. As I got into the car, an emotional weight fell off of me. I had escaped their banter and was headed toward my purpose.

As I drove, many questions occupied my mind. *What kind of church will this be? Will the people be friendly? Will I like the pastor? Will the people like me? What a gorgeous day.*

I was trying to put my finger on the unfamiliar impressions that were swirling around inside me. *Innocence, that's it. I feel innocent, hopeful, and excited.* I just knew that my imaginary *great life* was about to be a reality.

I parked the car and started walking toward the church. As I passed a few people, we exchanged greetings. I stepped inside the small church near the back of the auditorium and before I had a chance to look around, I saw the pastor walking down the center aisle toward me. When he reached me, he held out his hand and said, "Well, hello there."

I felt my unconscious fatherlessness completely take over. He had a booming voice, a masculine look, and a firm handshake. He finished off his introduction with direct eye contact and a well-intentioned smile. He was just the right age to be my dad.

Did I just hit the mother lode? A Pastor, a Mentor, and a Father all in one?

I told him my name and we spoke for a few minutes. He introduced me to a few people and then I took a seat one row back from the front on the left side. One reason I remember where I sat is because I had sat on the right my entire life — and it was time for a change.

It was a small but willing congregation. The only musician was a piano player. The minute the singing started, I was raptured. For people who have never had the experience, it is hard to explain. It's an experience of being in the now, where the past and future only exist in the present.

I was so ready to walk down the path of the rest of my life. I believed, really believed, that I was embarking on a divinely appointed journey of discovery and fulfillment. I didn't want what was behind me. I wanted the promises ahead of me.

What I was hungry for, what I was thirsting after, was pouring over me like rain. I got a little lost, like I was the only one there. I could hear the other people, but it was more like white noise to facilitate my rest. The experience of worship didn't wear off for some time. In fact, I recall very little of the rest of the service that day.

I was stepping out of the door after the service when I was invited to the pastor's house for lunch. I quickly agreed, as I was eager for new friends.

The pastor and his wife had a beautiful home. They had two daughters, and a young son that attended the church. One girl was a few years older than me and the other one was a couple of years younger. The younger daughter was the piano player and worship leader. All appearances indicated a great family. I enjoyed the meal and the interaction at the table. After lunch, the two girls took me to play tennis. It was a fun-filled afternoon and we enjoyed a lot of laughs. After a short rest, we headed back to church for the Sunday evening service. It was a great day.

On the way back to the base and barracks that night, I thought about the last church family I got close to and how badly that had ended.

It's going to be okay. I'm in a different place now. I'm committed to the ministry.

The next several months were bountiful with much learning, growing, and developing. I performed my military duties during the week, but impatiently waited for the weekend activities built around church life. I bonded with my new pastor, spending time with him away from church. He did construction work, and I was able to do some work with him. I liked the father-son aspect of our relationship.

His piano-playing, worship-leading daughter and I also became friends. We liked each other. A lot. After some time, we entered a dating relationship. She was my first bona fide girlfriend. I believed in her. She believed in me. And we believed in a life together. We were young and inspired with virgin dreams. After about a year, I asked her to marry me and she said, "Yes."

It was a picturesque day in Southern California. This Sunday would be a landmark day, as we would speak to her father after morning service. I must admit to being a little distracted during the service with anticipation and nervousness about talking to the pastor. I tried to focus, but I couldn't help rehearsing my lines and envisioning how I would begin the big conversation.

When the service was over and most everyone had left, I asked if we could speak to the pastor privately, and we were led into his very small office. He sat down, and we continued to stand.

"What are the two of you up to?"

"I want to ask for your daughter's hand in marriage," I belted out.

He offered a warm smile that released all the tension in the room. "I have been thinking about that," he said, "and I'm not surprised. I give you my blessing. And, I don't mind having you for a son."

Wait, did he just affirm me as a son? I didn't know what to be more excited about, him saying yes to our marriage or his fatherly inclinations.

We walked out of his office on the proverbial "cloud 9." We were in love and had the giggles, too. My life felt right. It really felt right. I had the joy of today and the promise of tomorrow. I believed my life was on track and full of purpose and direction. I had met the girl I wanted to marry. We shared the same dreams and aspirations. God did have plans for me and they were good plans!

I was no longer facing the painfully dark clouds of abandonment, rejection, and molestations. The relentless chatter of *you're not enough* and *you're not good enough* suddenly seemed to have a severe stuttering problem. The recorded lyric of *you're too messy to love* had lost its power. I had a new day and a new song. I was seeing myself in a new way. I was off to the races with the belief that I could win.

Within minutes, it all changed. Her mom was not happy. In fact, she was adamantly opposed to our marriage. Within hours, we were called in and given the news that our engagement would have to be put on hold. I was told that her mom had a dream husband in mind for her daughter and I wasn't it. My upbringing wasn't like hers. Mine was messy. I thought my destructive inner chatter was gone, but there it was, in teeming regalia. I had already heard, "That's not my son." Now I was hearing, "That's not my son-in-law." And again, "You're too messy to love."

It was like an angry vacuum sucked all the life out of me. I spent months and months trying to be the person this woman would find worthy of her daughter, while all true learning and personal development ceased. One humiliation after another. Darkness replaced the light in my heart as I tried, yet again, to be good enough.

This romantic relationship, which had been pure, innocent, and full of infatuation, buckled under the pressure. As I wrestled with the idea that I was good enough for God but not good enough to marry this girl, I became confused and distraught. My internal campaign manager wrote a new speech, *Who do you think you are you dirty, little, fatherless bastard? You will never be worthy enough for good things!*

I was left at the altar. I had been taught the altar was the place where the sinner took his mess. When you saw yourself—your horrible, not enough, less than, unworthy self—you went to the altar to receive forgiveness and God's love. A steady diet of shame and fear drove me again and again to the same old place, where I confessed over and over how unworthy I was.

I was told the altar is where God washes you clean, wipes out your past, and you are born again. I was told you are granted a new life. I thought I had achieved legal standing in this matter. I believed I had attained this highly desirable status. I was conducting my life, in good faith, based on the notion that things were right between me and God. Now, because of another mother-figure's determination that I was not worthy, I found myself back at the altar with nothing more to say.

This was a setback that penetrated deeply into my soul. I instinctively believed that at the altar, you would find the unsearchable riches of God's treasures — God's place for me and plan for my life. I had an open heart, which was fully enticed to believe that God would not withhold any good thing from me. But somehow I was disqualified. I appeared to be permanently assigned to the altar where I could only perpetuate my pain and sorrow.

And who am I to argue with this woman and her husband, who hold positions of such authority in these matters?

Hopelessness sent me into deep personal despair.

If all I have to look forward to are continuous confessions of unworthiness at the altar, I should just end things right here and now. If I'm never going to be good enough, then what is the point?

I felt like the church had brought God to meet me. I thought He had asked for me by name. I felt like I had sat on his lap for a couple of hours. I thought we had played, laughed, and bonded together. I believed He meant it when He said He would always be there for me. His promises were profoundly imprinted on my inner thoughts. God was there. He was real. I had experienced Him. But He just wasn't there for me. I could no longer see Him. I wondered if I would I ever see Him again...

Just like my father!

With the life beaten out of me, I left the church, imagining that I could leave the disapproval behind. I thought I would just move on by attending another church. Then I ran into another unhappily married woman and had another affair. More mess at only twenty years of age.

I heard the lyric, and I danced to the tune. I took my heartbreak and moved on. Now my faith was shaken. God had always been the "go to" in the back of my mind. With the mindset of shattered faith, I was about to find out just how *messy* things can get.

Jaden was snuggled up to my side as we sat on the cool leather sofa. The sun was going down and what light it had left was gently being sent to us through the double paned windows. A shadow was cast across half of the room.

It was an easily phrased question and it rolled off of his lips, "Papa, if I do well on my homework, will you be proud of me?"

Knowing exactly where this question came from and where it could lead, I framed my response with care.

I drew him up to see his face. I paused to take in his beautiful eyes and his warm smile. I wanted him to see the beam of love in my facial expressions.

"Jaden, I am proud of you, right now, before you do your homework. I love you without you having to earn it. My love for you isn't attached to how well you do something. You don't have to do anything for me to love you and be proud of you. Doing things well is how we *express* love, not how we *get* love. You are enough,

Jaden, right now and always. I am so filled with love for you, and I am so proud of you, that every time I see you all I can say is, 'That's my boy!'"

You Are Unique

You must know from where you came,
For here and now you are the same.
As you find wisdom from far and wide,
Know all you will ever have comes from inside.

You are not meant
To be like another.
It is knowing why you were sent
That will take you further.

In your circumstances you are to rise,
Allowing no one to diminish your size.
It is not a halo that you will need,
It is in your connection your spirit will feed.

Every single day, find the laugh, the cry,
and the celebration,
And you will never want for an alternate destination.
When you keep your heart open and fill the arena,
You will not have to answer to a divine subpoena.

When you have found your own beat and dance,
The whole world will want more than a casual glance.
Don't be shy and deny anyone a peek,
Your contribution to others, comes from being unique.

Chapter 5

I Honor Your Unique Personality!

My smile was waiting for me when I woke up. It was Christmas time, my favorite holiday, and Jaden had arrived the night before to spend his school break with us. I peeked in, and he was still fast asleep. I gave myself just a few moments to admire him, not wanting to disturb his rest. His clock was two hours behind us, and he arrived pretty late. Then I kept him up as long as I could.

I can be patient a little longer. His smile, greeting, and hug will be worth the wait.

I walked on air to the kitchen. I got out my coffee cup and pour-over brewer, set the pot of water on the stove, turned on the burner, hit the button on the coffee grinder, and waited for that great cup of morning joe. As I waited for the water to boil, I checked the hall to see if my boy was stirring.

The coffee smelled fantastic, and I was looking forward to my first sip as I positioned myself on the maroon love seat. This was not where I normally sat, but it gave me the best view to see Jaden when he came out of the bedroom. I had the table lamp on low. I used a folding dinner tray to set my coffee on so I could celebrate Jaden without being encumbered.

After my second cup of coffee, I heard the door open, and out came my long-haired grand boy, rubbing the sleep from his eyes and partially shielding himself from the light. I got up on my feet to do my papa jig and sing, "That's my boy! That's my boy!"

If I had of known how much pure joy was involved in being this grand boy's papa, I would have had him much sooner.

Even though he was barely awake, he couldn't resist, and released his show-stopping smile. I sat back down on the love seat just as he reached me. "Hi, Papa."

"Hi, Grand Boy. Did you get enough sleep?" I picked him up and set him on my lap.

"Yes," he replied. "What are we going to do today?" he asked, turning to look up into my face.

"What do you want to do?" I looked back.

"Can we go to Chuck E. Cheese?" he asked with wide eyes.

"You bet we can," I answered with equally wide-eyed excitement.

"Yeah!" he exclaimed.

I am a contented man, I thought to myself, as I took in every feature of this amazing kid.

"We should talk about getting your hair cut," I stated.

"No! No haircut!" he shouted. His mother always likes his hair longer than what seems reasonable for a little boy. I think manageability trumps style, and the last time we were together, it was quite the effort to get a comb through his hair.

Okay, bribery is allowable for grandparents, right?

We made the deal for just a trim. On the drive over to the hair shop, Jaden was asking questions of just about everything he saw. This was his first trip to Texas and everything was new to him. We pulled into the parking lot of the strip mall and headed inside.

As Jaden was climbing into the technician's chair, I explained that we only want a trim. The stylist started to put the cape on Jaden when I noticed tears were flowing down his cheeks. Thinking he might have gotten hurt somehow, I asked, "What's wrong, Jaden?"

"I don't want to get my hair cut, Papa."

My heart stopped. I apologized to the nice lady, but I couldn't get Jaden out of that chair fast enough.

I knew we were not talking about hair at that point. I knew it was something more. And, I was eager to find out just what it was this five-year-old was experiencing. Standing outside of the hair shop, I knelt down to hug Jaden to reassure him that this was okay with me. "Did you make a deal with me that you really didn't want to make — just to get the rewards I offered?"

He nodded through the tears pouring from his big brown eyes.

After I apologized and explained that I was partly having fun with him because we were going to do those things anyway, I wiped the tears from his cheeks. We walked to a metal bench, with wooden slats, and sat down.

"Jaden, this is a really good lesson for Papa to share with you. Don't ever make deals that you don't want to make. Not even with Papa. Not with anyone. Most importantly, don't make deals you don't want to make with yourself. What you just did is what I want you to always do. Check your heart before you say *yes* or *no* to anything."

This was my attempt to explain, to a five-year-old, the importance of never selling out.

The power of choice is an inspired attribute, securely planted in the cavernous recesses of our very being. Life is a celebration. To adopt an environment of toleration is to dishonor our own life. And this is how it begins. The subtle impulse to step aside from our unique identity to gain approval from someone else. I need him to understand that I will help guide, but not control, his life.

He had snuggled up close, as the wind was getting a little nippy. I wanted to know the real reason he cried. "Can you tell me why you don't want to cut your hair?"

He said, "Can we talk about it in the car, Papa? I'm getting cold."

All buckled in, we pulled out of the parking lot and Jaden answered, "I don't want to cut my hair because

I get a lot of compliments about my hair. Everybody loves my hair the way it is. But if I cut my hair, they might not like me anymore."

Aha!

I knew that concern well. In fact, that's exactly the reason I had worked so hard for my worthiness to win the girl when her mother refused to give me her hand in marriage. And that deal I made with her, and the deal I made with myself against my own conscience, led me to some of the darkest moments of my life.

It was a rare, rainy day in southern California and my wipers were barely keeping pace. As I drove down the highway, I was dealing with an equally gloomy, stormy heart.

The last six months had been intense with rejection and shame. I wanted to be freed from the constant messages of *"you're not wanted; please go away,"* and, *"you will never be good enough or worthy enough."* I had pressed very hard toward the life I desired, and it had come to a crippling outcome.

I was backing away from my life, and my dream, so that someone else could have theirs.

With only three months left before I would be discharged, I was under a lot of pressure to reenlist from my superiors. Not realizing that something inside me had switched to the off position, I made the decision to serve another three years and I was sorry immediately.

But it was too late. I was on the run and headed for a tour of duty in Brunswick, Maine.

Dejection took up the most space in my car as I tried to take in the landscape between San Diego and Maine. I had never seen Arizona or New Mexico, and I was looking forward to taking in the sights, as much as I could, from the car. The farther I got from California, the more I felt like I was going in the wrong direction. Every emotion possible was making the trip with me.

This is not what I want! This isn't even Plan B. This is the parachute I grabbed on the way down, hoping to break my fall.

I began to grasp the fact that I had sentenced myself to three years in exile.

In the far-off distance of my awareness, I perceived that I had been dishonored, and instead of appropriately repositioning myself, I had come into agreement with it. That little voice inside that had tugged on my heart since I was ten years old seemed like it had vanished into thin air. I had a feeling of emptiness that was beginning to weigh more than I could carry. Two years of dedication, learning, and developing appeared to have been for nothing. I had walked away and abandoned the things and the people that had once given me the most hope.

If only I had a dad...

Every time I needed wisdom and guidance, I went to this place of solitude, desiring comfort from someone that had never been there to give it. I wanted to change my mind. I wanted to go back. I wanted to tell the military that I had made a mistake.

But what would I go back to? Especially now that I know even the people of faith are going to make me try to prove that I'm worthy...when I'm not even sure that I am.

The same dysfunction I was raised with was the same dysfunction I had experienced in my religion. Knowing I could not change anything, I kept my foot on the accelerator. With a craving for deeper spiritual meaning, I just continued on.

Driving by oneself, for hours on end, provides ample time to be alone with one's thoughts, and all of their confusing meanderings.

I thought I had something to offer. I really felt like I had contributions to make. Yeah, right. Who do you think you are?

Mile after mile, across the varied terrains of the country, the two sides of my being squared off with one another, and I wondered which side would win.

It was my twenty-first birthday, and I was approaching the Maine state line in a full-blown blizzard. The wind was blowing snow across the road and making it difficult to see. Swirling snow funnels reminded me of tornados. I barely saw the sign that said, "Welcome to Maine." The roads were slick, icy, and dangerous.

"What have you done to yourself?" I asked myself out loud as I peered through the window, trying to find my way to my new home.

For the next three years, I answered that question in the most self-betraying ways possible.

I took my deep God-given appetite for spiritual things and turned away from His face. I pursued — with great zeal — ways to not think or feel anything associated with what I believed I was on earth to do and be.

It hurts too much to imagine that I'm supposed to be a spiritual leader, but that I will never be deemed worthy enough to do what I'm here to do.

I learned to drink, and it became a serious problem as I mixed alcohol with inner turmoil and pain. It was a practice that offered temporary distraction, but would eventually deliver long-term negative consequences.

I worked out and buffed up, hanging out in places where men sometimes wanted to test their manhood by physical altercation. I figured out how to defend myself. I got good enough at it to develop a reputation — which I learned was just as valuable as skill itself. Men thought twice before they would challenge me. That meant I only had to face the occasional gunslinger, wanting to beef up his own reputation.

My popularity was sufficient to provide plenty of acquaintances, but true friendship did not come easy for me. I could be the life of the party. I was good for laughs, thrills, and a touch of danger. But people had no idea that I was often sitting on those bar stools, thinking about things that would make for good sermons. I even thought about sending my ideas to my ordained uncle so he could develop them. My destiny was present... but not believed enough to save me from the life I was reactively creating.

Up to this point, I had only experienced minor success with girls. I had done much better with married women for some reason. But once I figured out how to be enticing, things changed rapidly. Since the military club was the largest and most popular club in the area, it was standing room only most of the time. There were so many girls, you could fall in love nearly every day if you wanted to. Many of the girls were hoping to find the love of their life, but I was just trying to survive. And it didn't help that at my core, I had a hard time respecting and trusting women, thanks to my mother and a few other ladies.

The mask I wore and the make-believe life I managed got more and more expensive to maintain. I might have appeared original, but I was far from authentic. Everybody wants to have a good time. Everyone wants love and affirmation. Some people never define what that looks like. I knew what I wanted and what it looked like. But I was drowning in the idea that I was somehow disqualified from ever having it. Feeling like I had been assigned to an inescapable under-worthy class of persons, I was ignoring the unique me.

Every five or six weeks, I would take a short reprieve from my artificial life and sneak off to church. It was a large enough congregation that I could come and go and not have to interact. I would cry, weeping like a baby with colic, through most services, and then exit as quickly as I could. The pastor was able to corner me on a few occasions, but I wouldn't even think about committing to faith again. All I wanted to do was see, in my state of confusion, if God was still there. See if I could still see the lighthouse through the fog and darkness. If

He was still detectable, that would be a safe-house in the middle of my distortion.

It would take more than the usual invitations of "God loves you and has a place for you" to reignite spiritual passion and turn me toward the Light. I had turned to my faith for affirmation. I had presented my unique personality, offered my gifts and talents, and it didn't work out. I believed that God had let me down. But, I was muddled by the abiding inclinations I had. I wanted to believe that I had encountered the failures of people and not the failure of God. But I couldn't separate the two.

I didn't know how driven I was. How large of a spiritual appetite I had. And I was learning the hard way that one can go just as passionately in the wrong direction as they can the right direction. I assumed the false identity of hyper-masculinity. Instead of helping myself and other people, I became self-destructive. And if you were in my proximity, it was easy to get caught up in my whirlwind.

In those moments when I was alone, and the lights weren't flashing, and the music wasn't blaring, I could hear the faint whisper of clarity beckoning me to see that what I wanted was already with me. I knew I wanted off the rollercoaster. Anger, disappointment, rejection, wrong thinking, and unbelief had me wrapped in layers of detrimental outcomes.

I was following the thoughts my feelings created and not using my thoughts to create my feelings. It had been that way from the start. I felt like some worthy person's dream had shown up in my heart by mistake. I had a fatal case of *trauma drama,* which had me in a starring role in the production of my own *divine comedy.*

In my consciousness, I rejected the internal chatter of not being good enough or worthy enough. But, in my subconscious, I had terrifying agreement rooted in my inner sanctum. I believed that deep inside, in the solace of my private harbor, I bore foundational errancy. When no one was looking and I was out of earshot, I was begging for merciful deliverance. Because I was distraught over the missing voice of the father that wasn't there, I missed the voice of The Father that was.

The whisper of divinity would reach an ear-piercing decibel before I would know who was talking to me.

It was one of the three annual good days of weather in Maine (partially joking) — warm, not muggy, with clear skies and fresh air. I started early, intoxicating myself. My roommates eventually joined me and a few more friends showed up as the day went on. Somewhere in the night, I crossed over and went too far.

As I looked out from behind the bars, I wasn't quite sure about everything that was happening around me.

Suddenly significant people from my social circle began to show up. When my executive officer appeared, I began to think that maybe I was in real trouble. He told me not to say anything and that he would see about getting me released. The longer time went on, the more I grew concerned. I could see conversations taking place, and when I read the displeasure on the faces of my friends, fear gripped my soul.

What was a very stupid act on my part — *After all, what's a few bullets among friends?* — was going to be made into a big deal.

My attorney believed one or more police officers thought they could make a reputation off my unfortunate actions. I was transferred from the city jail to the county facility. As I sat in the back seat of the police cruiser, in handcuffs, I sobered up expeditiously, doing my best to resist sheer panic.

The county jail felt desolate and remote, even though it was in Maine's largest city. The processing room where I was taken was small and confined. The intake procedures were invasive and violating. Humiliation was manipulating my insides. I outlived the process and was taken to a small cell where I was locked up alone. There was no window in the cell. There was a solid metal bunk, with no mattress or pillow, and a thin blanket to cover myself. A toilet sat in the corner, and a tiny overhead light was secured behind a metal shield, which completed the cold and uninviting accommodations.

The steel door shut with the slam of isolation. The uncanny sound of the key as it slid into the lock, and the sinister noise of the bolt as it snapped into place, took away my freedom and left me covered in chills. I sat down on the bunk, in the stillness of the darkness, and stared into the abyss that I had recklessly crafted.

How did this happen? How did I get here? This is definitely not the life I want. Where's my dad?

"God, we have to talk."

The next few days were the longest of my life and the nights were even longer. I expected some information about formal charges and getting out on bail, but no information came. I paced back and forth, three steps one direction and two and a half steps back, which was the extent of my daily travels. I thought about the precious childhood that never was and the innocent dreams of a young man that were discarded as waste. I heard screams, night after night, that sounded like someone was being attacked.

"God, we really have to talk."

Five days later, I was released on bond. The charges were the most serious they could file. I had made my roommate dance in the driveway as I fired a .22 rifle at his feet...in a residential area. Someone could have gotten hurt or worse. But, attempted murder was a bit of a stretch. Legal proceedings were protracted beyond my military service, so I was honorably discharged; and then I dealt with my judicial woes. A plea deal followed quickly, which demonstrated how political it all was to begin with. I plead guilty to assault, received probation, and moved on.

This was a big wake-up call. Armed with fresh determination to find my path, I began to chart myself a different course.

Mature thoughts will change you. When rejection is not harnessed to stay within the borders of accurate interpretation, it can evolve into something much more complex. I thought I was dishonored because I deserved it. I had lived down to my expectations and tragedy had followed.

Released, I headed for the General Conference of the denomination I was raised in, which was being held in Philadelphia, Pennsylvania. As I navigated unfamiliar highways and drove through town after town, I was in continual reflection. I had a lot of soul-searching to do. I pulled into the city of brotherly love during rush hour. With cars passing and honking their horns at me, I didn't feel any love as I tried to find my exit.

In the middle of traffic-rich congestion, I had a heartfelt talk with God. "I don't want to fail again," I said out loud. "If this isn't going to work this time, just let me die on this highway, please."

I had been in San Francisco for a few days enjoying some wonderful quality time with Jaden. I was experiencing some sorrow knowing I was leaving later that day. My grand boy was not yet awake. I laid next to him just watching him sleep. My heart was filled with love. I gently touched his thick hair and rubbed his precious arm. Deep emotion overcame me and tears began to flow. I worried that the intensity of my tears would wake him. In part, I was grieving over my own life, but in a deeper sense, it was to protect his life.

For the better part of an hour, I stayed in divine contemplation.

Who is Jaden and what will he do with his life? He must know his value. He must know that he is deserving of the best life possible.

I bound myself to his journey, and I vowed to do my part — to give him the affirmation, love, and sense of worthiness necessary to reach unlimited heights.

The bedroom window was open. The noise of traffic was prevalent. There was a siren in the background. The city was already bustling with activity.

I want life for Jaden. The characteristics of father-lessness have already revealed themselves in this precious boy.

With tears still rushing from my eyes, I reaffirmed my mission to provide nurturing, guidance, and support for his wings, wisdom, and wonder.

My whole life seemed to be flashing through my mind.

I am certain that being Jaden's grandfather is by divine design. I have never known the kind of love I have for this boy, and I am grateful beyond words. Every struggle I have ever faced, and every dark day I have ever endured, every failure where I rose from the ashes, and every victory I have ever achieved has been for this moment in time.

The purest, most majestic, and unadulterated view of God I have ever experienced happened when I held Jaden in my arms and looked into his eyes for the very first time.

The plight of fatherlessness vanished from my mind.

My story of separation, disconnection, violation, rejection, and abandonment is being rewritten to reflect a more accurate accounting.

As I smiled at the long hair tangled on his pillow, I whispered my intention that he would never feel like he had to be anyone other than who he is. "Jaden, as you grow more into expressing your unique personality, I want you to see clearly. I want you to honor and reverence the gift of life. I want you to hear and recognize the voice of guiding inspiration that lives inside of you. I want you to know where you came from and where you are going. I want you to own your heart. I want you to be able to identify the efforts, from outside influences that attempt to wrap you in inadequate definitions. You, my grand boy, are not here to be someone else. You are *made* unique, there's nobody like you!"

Life is about discovery. It took too long, at least longer than it should have, for me to realize that before the ultrasound shows life in the womb, the intangible organs of love, worthiness, and acceptance are present.

"If people fail to confirm your value, Jaden, let it be your instructor to show you a better way. Don't let anyone define you. Let no one design your life. Allow only confirmation of what you know for certain. You came from uniqueness. There is nothing wrong with you. The day you accept your unique perfection, you will know who you are. And, you will know The Father!"

Wherever You Go

Don't run and hide to stand naked in your socks,
My heart is not pious to gasp in shock.
I already know what you might want to tell.
Between me and you, things are well.
Wherever you go, I am with you.

Your little imperfections I don't mind.
Don't live in fear to let life unwind.
Always avoid sitting down at the table
Where they ask you to devour some inappropriate label.
Wherever you go, I am with you.

You may seek things that are not hiding.
It might even feel like you're a bit off-track.
But when you see my love and protection abiding,
You will find my provision built into your pack.
Wherever you go, I am with you.

It is fine that you walk thru deep-seeded doubt.
I do not fold my arms to sit in anger and pout.
I turn up the music and ask you for a dance
And teach you the steps of love's great balance.
Wherever you go, I am with you.

As you divide darkness from the Light,
You will see the journey is grace, love, and delight.
It is not treachery that I demand you swallow
But a sacred path I created for you to follow.
Wherever you go, I am with you.

And when you return safely to your abode,
With scars and from ashes you will have arose.
Your free-flowing smile will mate with mine,
As you take in the revelation that I am there all the time.
Wherever you go, I am with you.

Chapter 6

I'm With You Wherever You Go!

Jaden's mother couldn't get him enrolled in class in San Francisco, so the decision was made to let him stay with us and attend his first year of preschool. I was in my own land of enchantment. My emotional high was too abundant to be legal. Shopping for school clothes and getting him a backpack was over-the-top fun. He was such a big boy, showing great courage, when he went to school that first day. His attitude was totally, *I got this!*

Throughout the year, Jaden declared, "This is my home. I'm not going back to San Francisco." In fact, he told his mom she needed to move back to Indiana with us if she wanted to be with him. I think Monica was suspicious of papa-manipulation, but he was expressing his own feelings. And, there was no way I could force him to go back.

When Monica came out for his graduation, she still hadn't found a school in her area to accommodate her work schedule. I was certain we would be talking about him staying another year or her moving back to Indiana. I knew he needed his mom, but I couldn't stand the thought of him leaving again.

Tina, Monica, and I were sitting in our living room when Jaden came in, sat next to his mother, and said, "Mom, I have been thinking about something for a long time, and I have made a decision. When you leave, I'm going to go back to San Francisco with you." My heart sank. I had no idea he was thinking and feeling this way. I was not only shocked by what he was saying, but stunned by how he was saying it.

Monica hadn't planned to take him back right then, so she said, "Baby, I didn't know you wanted to come back. Mommy has to make plans for you to come home. I can't take you right now, but I will work it out so you can come soon."

With sadness, he responded, "I had this all worked out, and you're messing up my plan."

His mom apologized again, reiterating that she would go home and make plans for him to come as soon as possible. He said, "Okay," with acceptance and disappointment.

I think we might be raising the next Einstein.

A couple of months later when Monica came to get him, I was a wreck. I was so mad at her for not moving back. As a single mother with a fatherless child, I thought she should realize just how much she needed our support and he needed us.

I know she is entitled to her own life, but it makes my ability to be involved in Jaden's life so difficult! I knew I would need to navigate the distance with deliberate intention.

It was a wonderful summer day with the overcast reality that Jaden was leaving. I was decomposing, trying to extract every bit of joy out of my last few moments with him, and he was acting like it was just another day. I was beginning to think this genius just didn't get it. His papa was dying inside. We loaded the bags in the car. I put Jaden in his carseat, and strapped him in like I had done so many times. Only this time, I was moving in slow motion.

We pulled out of our driveway and headed to the airport. The sun was shining, and I was in despair. I had never prayed for a traffic jam or flight cancellation, but I was now.

Anything to keep my grand boy with me!

No such luck. We got inside the terminal and waited for their departure. The last time Jaden left, he was holding on to my leg crying, because he didn't want to go. His mother had to pry him away and carry him to the plane. This time he just said, "Bye, Papa," gave me a kiss and hug, and off he went.

We waited until they were out of sight before we turned and walked away. I was a mass of dwindling manhood. I was bawling, and I didn't care who saw it.

I wanted to throw myself down in the middle of the airport and pitch a fit. We got out of the parking garage and onto the highway. I was trying to drive through the blurry waterfalls pouring from my eyes, hoping to not crash the car. We made it home safe and sound, and I went straight to the couch and hurled myself into it for an extended period of serious moping. I just wanted the world to let me sulk in peace.

Several hours later, my cell phone rang. I knew the kids hadn't landed in California yet, and I didn't want to talk to anyone, so with hesitation I picked up the phone. When I saw that it was Jaden calling on Facetime, I dropped the phone and almost disconnected the call. I hit the button and Monica's distraught face appeared on the screen. "Dad, you're going to have to talk to Jaden. He started crying as soon as the plane pushed back from the gate, and he has cried all the way to Dallas." They were changing planes there.

Monica held the phone so I could see him, and my heart hurt at the sight of him. I had never seen him cry so hard. He was inconsolable. "Papa, I want to come back. I made a mistake, Papa. I want to come home. Please, Papa." I was in no condition to be encouraging, but I had to find a way to dry his tears. His pain was heartbreaking.

"I love you, Grand Boy. You're going to have a good time being with Mommy. When you get home, you will have fun with all the toys you have there. Jaden, I am always with you wherever you go. When you miss Papa, just put your hand on your heart and Papa is right there with you." He slid his hand up and placed it on his heart, and I continued. "Whenever you miss Papa, just remember all the fun we have had and think about all the fun we will have when we're together again. You're in Papa's heart, and I'm in your heart; so we are always together."

"Okay, Papa, but I still want to come back," he sniffled.

I told him that I would come to San Francisco to see him real soon.

If only I had realized the truth that, like Jaden, I was never alone...

After attending the big conference in Philadelphia, I was once again loaded with expectancy about my future. Since I seemed to get off-track when I walked away from my church in California, I concluded that I needed to re-enter where I had exited. I took responsibility for all failings. It had to be my fault. The mother declaring me unworthy, the Pastor and father letting it happen, I assumed blame for all of it. Focused on getting my life together and pursuing my dreams of ministry, I set my sights for California. I cannot say I didn't have a distant notion about a possible lost love in the back of my mind, but I didn't know the status of my former girlfriend, or if she would even still be interested.

I can't think about that right now. I have the same root issues I had three and a half years ago — with more layers of consequences and complexity.

I experienced the love of a son toward a father, and I believed the pastor was the man to help facilitate my rehabilitation. After all, he was one of the few who had made me feel like a son.

Don't worry about the past, I told myself. *Just lean forward. Good things are ahead!*

It had only been a few months, but I was trying to follow the whisper inside me. I launched in, full-speed ahead, to pick up where I left off. I flourished.

I want this. I can do this. I know I can.

I cleaned the church, taught classes, and fumbled around learning to speak publicly. Inspired thoughts captured my mind. And I wrestled with that gentle voice inside. It tried desperately to provide the wisdom I was searching for, but I was still blocked in my understanding.

A year later, I found myself in familiar territory. The girl was still there, our interest was still there, and her mother's opposition was still there. Once again, I went to work to earn my worthiness. I should have learned my lesson. But I was failing, one more time, to keep my inner chatter from cluttering my life.

Approval addiction is as fierce as any substance abuse. *Like me, accept me, affirm me,* and *love me* drove me like a stalled jet in a free fall. I didn't feel good about me and I was desperate for someone else to, especially those who had rejected and shamed me. I imagined how good it would feel if they changed their minds and wanted me.

I knew what I wanted, *I believed.* I knew how I was going to get it, *I thought.* I was incorrectly determined. I was in the wrong place, heading in the wrong direction, hoping the right thing would appear.

Surely, titles and positions will rectify my misfortunes. If I can only achieve enough, I will be whole, right?

But my wounds were in the lead, not an open heart. My lessons were still coming from fear. It wasn't from joy that I was learning; it was from pain.

One day, the pastor sat me down and let me know it was time for me to head out on my own as a traveling evangelist. "I'm going to make some calls to help you get started with some speaking engagements. Rick, if you will pray and fast, I know you will make it just fine."

I wanted to believe that this was a meritorious promotion that came quicker than should be expected, but in my heart I knew I was not being sent out — I was being sent away (to separate their daughter and me). I lost respect that day for many of the things I had believed in. It would take some time before I would understand how deeply this affected me.

I'm not ready! I still have major internal work to do! The last time I left this church, I embarked on a journey that came close to killing me and a few others. At least this time, as fragile as it was, there was some direction with hope attached to it. *There has to be some way of moving on from this.* So I went stumbling into the unknown, thinking I still wasn't good enough to be wanted.

I made some new friends and, in spite of the many challenges I faced, I was actually having some fun for the first time in quite a while. Then, a phone call came as a surprise. It seemed the parents of the girl I'd wanted to marry had experienced a change of heart and asked me to meet with them.

I went to the meeting not really knowing what to think. But it only took a moment for me to realize nothing had changed, not really. The mother said, "I'm still against the two of you getting married. I think it will be a big mistake, but I'm not going to fight you anymore. You want to get married, go ahead."

In the time I'd been gone, I had met a nice young lady whose mother liked me and treated me with respect and common decency. There was no relationship at that moment, as we were just getting to know each other, but the two scenarios offered me a stark contrast, which I contemplated as I listened to what was being said and observed the tone, texture, and body language being displayed.

I am not willing to marry under these circumstances. I am no longer part of this church and all that it represents to me.

I wasn't over it all, of course, but I had to stand on my own ground. "You have put me through all of this stuff, for all of this time. Am I supposed to feel good about what you just said to me?" I knew the kind of wedding it would be. She would make sure nobody felt good about it. The ceremony itself would have been a miserable experience.

No, I had experienced enough of *"I don't want you"* from her. And just like that, I knew I would have to let this come to me if it was ever to be. A rare moment of wisdom accidently manifested in me, and I departed with some strength.

Miraculously, I landed on my feet at another church as an assistant pastor to a much larger congregation. I was elated to find a place to continue my growth. I knew I was in over my head, but I was determined to rise to the occasion. This pastor operated much differently, kept his distance. No father-son relationship was likely to develop there.

I am growing, but where is the peace?

After about six months on the job, I began making plans to minister across the country during a summer vacation, to visit my family in Rhode Island. With limited opportunities for places to speak, I thought of the pastor in Maine where I had periodically visited during my time there. I thought he would be excited for the direction my life was going and might be open to have me minister at his church. When I phoned his home, he wasn't there — but Tina was.

Tina? Whoa!

Tina was a girl I had dated sporadically during my three years in exile. Since we were not exclusive and our dating was very "on again, off again," I had plenty of doubts and questions when she became pregnant. Tina, on the other hand, had complete confidence that I was the father. Her resolve persuaded me to stand by her through the pregnancy.

At the time, I was in total discombobulation. My path of self-destruction had been interrupted with several monumental events — being discharged from the military, dealing with my legal troubles, and now the possibility of becoming a father. The lifestyle I had been engaged in the previous three years was directly opposed to everything I wanted. I was a walking contradiction, to say the least. Decisions had to be made; and while my heart was leaning toward California, I had to factor in the upcoming birth of this child.

My private hope was that the baby would look so much like me that all doubt would pass away. But that was not to be. Shannon was born with dark hair, big brown eyes, and olive-colored skin — a beautiful baby, but nothing like me. The nagging doubts, legitimate or otherwise, refused to let me be.

Even though Tina and I were not a couple, I sat down with her to explain why I had decided to return to California. As I tried to convey my deepest feelings and intentions for pursuing ministry, I mystified her. I had never spoken to her about this part of my life, and she wanted to know more about this God that had such a hold on me. I explained the best I could and put her in contact with the local pastor. We agreed that we would go our separate ways. I didn't see any other way.

I never thought Tina would follow through with exploring my faith; and yet, there she was, a year and a half later, attending that church and babysitting the pastor's children! I was stupefied…

We spoke briefly, catching up with each other. When I inquired about the baby, she described a precious child. I was overwhelmed with confusing emotions. I asked for pictures, and she graciously sent them.

I called the pastor a couple of days later, expecting to be warmly received, but was taken back by the tone of the conversation. He was disapproving of me being in ministry and shirking my responsibility to my child.

Wait! What? "My" child?

He went on to say he had a duty to call the pastor I was working under to let him know that I had a child I was neglecting.

Are you kidding me?

This sent cold chills of fear down my spine. I had not spoken about this situation to anyone, as I didn't believe I had any reason to. But I knew this could put me in a very bad light. And I feared the potential negative backlash could ruin me.

Suddenly on the defensive, I found myself trying to ward off this onslaught. I questioned the pastor about how much he knew of our past. "Can you assure me that I'm the father?"

"Well, uh, um, my wife has always said the baby has your eyes."

Seriously? Big brown eyes that look like my little green ones? This is the proof you have...the proof you would use to destroy my life and ministry?!?

I wanted to scream. Feeling vulnerable that yet another man was so ready and willing to discard me and my future, I was beside myself. Panic caused me to only see the negative.

Where does this end, God? When do I get to feel safe and accepted? Where are you?

True to form and out of panic, I resigned my position, removing myself from the threat of humiliation. Now there wasn't anyone the pastor would need to call to report me. And, I was alone to figure out why I was here again — dismissed, discarded, declared unworthy.

Even though I intuitively felt there was something incredibly wrong with this system of religion, my "less than" and "not good enough" self-image caused me to question and summarily dismiss my intuition that God was trying to lead me away from man-made concepts because He wanted to explain Himself to me. My faith was not fixing me and it continued to reinforce to me that there had to be something wrong with me. Believing in my own defect left me no choice but to continue to search for approval from other people to fill the void inside.

I needed identity, affirmation, and a sense of worthiness. Where was I going to get it?

Leaving California without saying anything to anyone, I ventured all the way across country, back to Maine. The more I thought about the possibility that I had done to my child what my father had done to me, the more it crushed me.

I wasn't abandoning my baby, I was trying to move forward in my life...and my calling. Without actually saying the words, "This is not my baby," I might have handed down to Shannon the gift that keeps on giving.

As I drove mile after mile, I recognized many sights that I had seen on my earlier trips; but my thoughts were focused on this child and what I needed to do to make things right. I was being eaten up with guilt.

Is marriage the right thing? I mean...now that Tina shares my faith, what reason could I possibly use for not...? And, you know, I've always wanted to be a father!

As I journeyed through the flat and mountainous terrains, I devised a plan. Without consulting Tina, I decided we should get married. Forget about the need to be in love. Disregard the necessity of compatibility and commonality. Trying to see only the good that could come from this situation, I didn't even consider that the lifelong dream I had of being in the ministry might be the last thing on earth Tina would want.

Again, the whisper, still and strong, tried to remove the confusion. *"You're moving too fast. It would be better to resolve outstanding issues before entering a marriage. You're making decisions out of fear and anger."*

It occurred to me that I should seek counsel on this. You know, the type of counsel a young man would seek from his dad...if he were around. I could have used his help, but I certainly wasn't going to ask this pastor who had threatened me for any assistance.

Even if I had someone to talk to, where would I start? Right or wrong, I was making decisions. I blew into town on a mission and I accomplished my objective. Marry the girl and leave.

I envisioned a happy reunion with Tina and a joyous meeting between father and child. I prayed that Shannon would instinctively recognize me as "Father." I was to meet Tina at her mother's house. Her mom and I liked each other and we spent some time chatting before they arrived. As we watched Tina getting out of the car, her mom cautioned me, "Don't be hurt if Shannon won't come to you right away."

Before even saying "Hello" to Tina, I knelt down in front of that beautiful child with dark hair and olive skin, held out my arms, and said, "Hi, Shannon, come to Daddy!" Without a hint of hesitation, Shannon came right to me. I was smitten, instantly!

Acting out of fear, shame, and a father's love, I proposed marriage. Tina, having true feelings for me, graciously accepted, thinking her prayers were being answered and her dreams were coming true. She had no idea of the mess of a man she had pledged to marry.

A door opened on my trip across the country when one of the churches I spoke at offered me an Associate Pastor's position. Realizing they thought of me as a single man, I shared with them that I was on my way to Maine and I might be getting married. They still wanted me to come. So, I made that a part of the plan.

I'll show everybody I can face responsibility. I will do the right thing and prove that I'm a man, that I'm enough.

And with that, I thrust myself and Tina into a whirlwind neither of us were prepared for. While we did have the makings of a beautiful story, my back-story proved troublesome. As the honeymoon faded and reality set in, I was even more conflicted and disconnected. My thoughts and emotions were still out of sync. *Have I done what I was afraid of doing all along? Did I incorrectly marry? Did I miss God's will for my life?*

I had attached serious layers of responsibility to an already congested immaturity. Positioning myself to perform publicly in ministry while struggling privately further strained my heavily taxed frailties. And Tina had been caught in my tornado. She had never thought of a life in ministry or even what that entailed. While, in my mind, she continually proved herself more than capable, she had her own feelings of being *less than* and *not enough* to battle with. Talk about a match made in... Well, let's just say, we didn't lack for challenges.

All the "second-guessing," coupled with my belief that marriage is permanent, had me spiraling. I was not only at odds with my faith, but with my very existence. I wrote stories around all these events that extended from my wrong beliefs and sense of unworthiness. Lies that I would live out as truth. I buried loose ends and unresolved issues, which set up like poorly poured cement that hardened with serious cracks. I was building on a foundation that was unsafe and would not hold.

I was begging for God's approval and love, He was pleading for me to see Him. I was asking, *God, where are you?* He was saying, *"I'm right here."*

I heard, *"Rick, stop trying to prove yourself. You'll never be any more than you are now. Don't be afraid. I'm not going to destroy you. I want you to know who I really am,"* in the background. But I was looking backwards trying to get ahead.

Without the confidence to believe what I was hearing, I remained detached from resolute healing. All I had was this one narrow opening into the possibilities of destiny and abundance as a minister. I simply could not let go of what I was holding on to because I could not see God any other way.

Questions emerged as I attempted to adhere to the tenets of my faith while witnessing regular abuses of power, territorialism, and inauthenticity. It all troubled me; and the further I went in my ministerial organization, the more disillusioned I became. The politics, nasty infighting, and god-players staggered my mind. Egos, human drive, deception, and lying were as prevalent as you would find anywhere.

How can we preach against these things when they seem to be going on everywhere I look?

Legalism, hypocrisy, and misrepresentations all existed in a culture of fear and manipulation.

We embed fear into people's hearts while telling them that God loves and wants to save them?

I just couldn't accept the error of it all. I could see it — I just couldn't believe it. And, I didn't know what to do with what I was seeing. I struggled to define and witness the love of God, as my experience qualified me only as an expert in what love is not. But in my heart, I didn't believe any of this represented a loving father.

But what can I do? Leave...the church? My purpose? My identity?

It was my own dysfunction that kept me playing the game. My core beliefs about myself prevented me from understanding the God I sought to know. My wrong thinking made me weary. I not only had God in a box; I had myself boxed in. I was trapped.

After five years of marriage, a second child, pastoring our first church, and several more verses of the same song playing over and over in my life and ministry, we were invited to work with a friend that pastored a successful church in another state.

Our first day there, Tina and I ran into my pastor friend's wife in the hallway. I greeted her and she didn't respond. Thinking she didn't hear me, I spoke again. It was the fourth and undeniable attempt before she forced herself to acknowledge us with a quick, unfriendly glance as she disappeared behind the door.

What's up with that?

Wisdom whispered, *"Load your family in the car and leave without saying a word."*

Not recognizing it for what it was, I ignored the voice and the generous protection it offered.

We settled in, and things took off. There were many high achievers in this congregation, and working alongside them, I experienced the kind of fulfillment that I had previously been unable to grasp. Elected youth president for the state shortly after arriving, I would now run the camps that I didn't get to go to as a kid, and many other things. My calling and my gift for preaching reached new heights, positively impacting countless lives; and my innate ability to move people forward thrilled me on so many occasions. I couldn't have been happier to be doing what I was called to do alongside some extraordinary friends and some of the superstars in my organization.

What an honor!

Even though my pastor friend was only ten years older than me, I quickly conceptualized him as a father. I thought, at first, we were both pleased with our relationship and the things we were accomplishing. And then...

What's going on here? Something's not right...

A mutual minister friend warned me about this pastor's jealousy toward me and strongly urged me to leave.

What? That doesn't make sense. He is more successful than I could ever be! Why would he be jealous of me? I dismissed his advice, not believing there could be any truth to it, refusing to believe this father-figure would do anything to hurt me.

But, soon after, our relationship deteriorated to an unsustainable situation. I was being blatantly manipulated and controlled, my Achilles heel. After being told of all the good things God had for me, my path to those things was being blocked. I was being sabotaged by the man who I had looked to as a father. Out of hurt and devastation, compounding the wound of abandonment and fatherlessness, I fought back. My disappointment was, perhaps, the deepest ever.

How can you preach to me what God has for me — mountaintops, significance, and power — and then aggressively work to prevent me from obtaining those things?

I had been down this path before. Much of the anger I thought I had overcome came back with a vengeance. I was raging.

But any disagreement with "dad" will always have a happy ending, right? Wrong!

As my wife and I sat at the conference table with our ministerial governing body (of which my friend was the newly elected leader), I was confronted with a truth. I had been summoned there with a concocted agenda to make me look bad. My friend had devised a plan to teach me a lesson for standing up to him: he would use his position and political connections to strip me of my title, my dignity, and my well-being. It seemed everyone in the room understood what was happening, disagreed with it, and yet allowed it to unfold without challenge.

Wisdom whispered, *"Lay your credentials on the table and remove yourself from this authoritative degeneracy."* The Father was there, trying to protect me, but I wasn't brave enough to do it. I didn't trust myself. I didn't know my value and my identity. I didn't understand my worthiness. I didn't know I mattered. My fatherlessness and lack of a secure identity still had me hobbled.

The next few days had me reeling and rocking with mental mayhem.

God, where are you? I know you are out there. I know you exist. I've experienced you! Why aren't you here for me? Tell me what to do...

I sought outside counsel from several esteemed elders and their advice was unanimous: "Pack up your family and head for safer ground."

I can't believe I'm being sent away again. Someday I'm going write a book entitled, "Going Away No More" — just as soon as I figure out how to stop going away.

My friend hit me hard enough emotionally that he looked exactly the same to me as my mom's husband when he knocked me unconscious. I did the only thing I knew how to do. I walked away. I returned to California bitter and broken. We slept on the floor in a friend's trailer for two months so our kids could sleep in a bed and I talked to myself, asking the same questions, over and over again.

How could this be happening inside the kingdom of God? Aren't You in charge here, God?

The betrayal was debilitating and left me lying wounded on the battlefield of my mind. For the next three years, I experienced recurring nightmares, often waking up in a sweat with chills. I was addicted to a religious identity that left me deluded. Seeking affirmation from an institution I did not respect took its toll on me. I kept things alive that needed to die. I remained committed to a path long after I was shown to get off of it.

Never being the quitter, I found new success, filling my schedule with speaking engagements but had to travel alone so Tina and the kids had stability. I wasn't being honest with myself. I wanted out of this environment. I knew God was much more than this culture allowed. Yet I didn't take the time to work through it all. I had established inadequate patterns for handling adversity. My methods permitted me to stay the course but provided no exit strategy. And everything felt messy.

My marriage was maxed out by my emotional turmoil and absence, and Tina was exhausted with the rollercoaster I'd pulled her onto. I missed my kids fiercely while I was on the road, and I didn't know how much longer I would be able to remain in such an erroneous religious institution.

Even still, there were signs that somehow, good could and would eventually come out of all the mess.

One day when I was on the road, I received shocking call: The woman I had relations with in Okinawa did have a baby, and it seemed I had a fifteen-year-old daughter that wanted to meet me.

Wow!

I had not heard from the woman since we said goodbye nearly sixteen years prior.

After all this time...I couldn't imagine this. I was so young when this took place, but felt the impact of having essentially repeated the pattern of fatherlessness that had devastated my own life. I called my wife to tell her what I just learned.

"Rick," she agreed, "you have to call. This is your daughter, and she might need you."

I had so many memories come rushing through my mind. As I walked back through the details of that period in my life, I twisted and stretched, trying to wrestle meaning out of this new development. With the unresolved issue of my own fatherlessness, I opened my heart to my newly-discovered daughter.

There were many questions, leaving me a little apprehensive, about what I might be walking into. I had no idea where the woman had been all these years. *What about her husband and the other children? Again, where's the certainty of paternity? How was she raised? How would my kids respond to having a sister they had never heard about? Would this change our lives significantly?* It was against that backdrop that I purposed to respond to a little girl who wanted to know her father.

I made the call and discovered that I have a wonderful daughter named Michelle. We met soon after, and she looks too much like me for there to be any questions. The story is complicated and yet there is love to stand on. I have a great son-in-law. And they have given me four beautiful granddaughters, and two great grandsons.

Sitting alone in my office, preparing my sermon for the Sunday evening service, I perceived what I call a holy hush. A divine pause. I was pastoring in the San Diego area. I was witnessing some more church politics, experiencing another display of rule-bending to suit people's agendas. I'd had enough of witnessing leaders' fire-breathing holiness toward others while exempting and justifying themselves. Putting together familiar scriptures and preparing to preach what I truly believed to be a misrepresentation, a failed interpretation, of God's intention, I declared out loud, "I don't believe this." I resigned the next Sunday, acknowledging I would never settle my own chaos within this context.

I finally came to the decision to part ways with the only organized religion and ministerial organization I had known. My heart let go of the culture many years before my hands let go of the structure.

I didn't know what I was going to do. I didn't plan well. I just knew I couldn't spend another minute in what I didn't believe was true, correct, or right. My organized religion was messier than I was. Once again, God was showing me things I just couldn't come to grips with. I still carried my unsettled issues, but God continued His efforts to guide my steps.

Everybody was responsible for my tales of woe. I blamed my mother and father, church and leaders, and everyone who had ever done me wrong. I had overcome a tremendous amount of adversity because I was strong, capable, and had some talents to rely on. But, I had levels of dysfunction that were treacherous. It was and is my responsibility to declutter my own life. In the end, what others have done, or have not done, doesn't matter. It's what *we do* that causes change.

I turned to insurance to make money. I grew a thriving business, took care of my family, and remained kind and helpful to others. I mentored and gave where I could. But I found myself in deeper pain. Being out of ministry was a complete loss of identity. I didn't like who I was as a preacher, and I really didn't like who I was not being a preacher.

I was enjoying success in my business but emptiness in my calling. And as I advanced in the secular, I recoiled from divine intention, making choices from pain. Whenever a father-type or a woman offered any counterfeit worthiness, I lost all of my better thinking and fell prey to my approval addiction.

I wandered around spiritually, trying to find a place to fit in. My issues of perceived separation from God intensified. Now that my only means of identity was gone, I shivered in anxiety.

Without the tools to resolve internal conflicts, I unhinged. Even though I had heard God tell me He simply wanted to love me, I couldn't imagine it. And why would I trust it? I held onto my stories of abandonment, neglect, rejection, and abuse tighter than ever.

The cracks in my foundation had given me much trouble over the years. My dysfunction kept me tied to a number of wrong behaviors. I would go long stretches of time without disruption, especially while I was preaching and seeing powerful results in congregations; but times of transition could set off self-destructive behaviors. I unconsciously used my pain to justify my inappropriate thoughts, attitudes, and actions. To ever be whole, I needed to deal with those cracks.

I never viewed my wife and marriage correctly. My love for Tina certainly grew over the years. Raising kids together and sharing life's ups and downs bonded us. But, the story I wrote about why and how we married kept me from being the man I wanted to be. In the early years, there were considerable obstacles. We had the normal adjustments to navigate — compatibility issues, communication problems, and learning to make decisions together. And, the added pressures of being in ministry where we were constantly under a microscope.

But underneath, I held on to something that had seeds of destruction in it. Even though I was the one who came to town planning marriage, I was never satisfied that I had found the so-called will of God concerning marriage. Putting this down on paper has the benefit of a backward look and analysis but does not reveal a consciousness at the time. This wasn't out in the open; it was deep inside me.

It had nothing to do with Tina. It wasn't about whether I married the right or wrong woman. It was about an abiding sense of unworthiness. It was about one rejection after another. It was about never resolving the way I was handled, the feelings of not being good enough. It was about being threatened and making decisions out of fear. I lived with doing things right, to be accepted, without being convinced I was doing the right thing. It was about me thinking something was wrong with me.

This kept an embedded wound festering. It kept my approval addiction vibrant. It kept me susceptible to the cycle of abuse and made me an abuser. I had to bring finality to the remnants of artificial living and an inauthentic life. I failed my kids by not loving their mother the way she deserved. And I had failed my wife by dishonoring her. No matter what it cost, there was only one thing for me to do to ever be whole.

It was then that I fell at her feet and confessed infidelity. This halted my knee-jerk reaction to look at what other people had done to me and forced me to face reality. I had broken someone else's heart and that was squarely on me. My brokenhearted living led me to devastate my wife. And that broke my own heart. What I did was far worse than anything that was ever done to me.

I had brought pain into my marriage and it resulted in unfaithfulness. The sheer terror of the things I had done wounded my wife terribly. It could have been the end of everything. I thought it was.

Everyone has always left me, or sent me away at the first notice of my messiness.

I offered to give her everything without a fight. I only wanted for her and the kids to be alright. I expected her to leave. Some women would have walked away. Maybe, for some, rightfully so. Tina made her own decision, out of strength, not weakness. She knew, even more than I did, that this wasn't me. The person who did these things was not who I am. My messiness was not me.

And in a moment where anyone else would have declared me "too messy to love," she stayed — giving me the first glimpse of the kind of love I had never been able to receive. I saw God in her eyes. Because of her, this broken boy could become a man.

There was no pat on the hand, I forgive you, don't do it again business. It was work. Hard work. She let go of my hand but cradled my heart. Because Tina is a behind-the-scenes person, few know her strength and wisdom. She provided a soft place for me to land, but made sure I walked on nails. I accepted responsibility for what I had done. I blamed only myself.

I sought help and answered the hard questions. It took time, energy, and focus. I read everything I could to identify the "why" for my decisions and behavior. The pain of my choices cut deep. Through therapy, where I explored my feelings openly (something I had resisted in the past), I began to see the truth of the lies.

I gave Tina reasons to distrust me. I had to own that. I jumped through hoops, made sure she didn't have anything to question concerning my whereabouts or who I was with. I communicated in a way that didn't leave her any room for thinking or feeling there was something she didn't know. I was able to love her the way she loves me.

Her love for me, her children, her God, and herself took center stage. The lessons of love and forgiveness she taught me restarted my maturation. Arrested development, legalistic doctrines, and self-destructive patterns no longer had a hold on me. I fixed it because she let me. We healed because we wanted to.

I was finally beginning to learn what love really is. Love sees who we really are underneath the mess of stories and lies and unhealthy patterns. Love calls us to be that person, and clean up the messes we've made. Love tells the truth. Love does not make us work to be worthy; it tells us that we already are and gives us the opportunity to act like it.

As I looked across the breakfast table, silently admiring my wife with a heart full of love, knowing with absolute certainty that I had always had the woman who is right for me, I wished that I could have understood my value, worth, and identity long before I let things happen. I wished I would have recognized and trusted that ever-present whisper.

All the time I was saying, If only my father was here... He was, and is...I just couldn't know it. He was talking to me, but I was so focused on proving my worth that I couldn't hear it. Love was present all along.

I had spent time with Jaden at a beautiful park in downtown San Francisco. It was a gorgeous day, and we had fun just hanging out. As we were walking home, Jaden asked, "Papa, am I your best friend?"

"You sure are!" I beamed.

"I mean, am I your number one best friend?" he coaxed.

"Yes, Jaden, you are my number one best friend!" I assured him.

"Will you always love me, Papa?" he asked the real question he'd been pondering.

"Yes, Jaden, Papa will always love you," I promised.

I recognized instantly what was going on in his mind. These are questions of the fatherless. These are the silent questions…behind the ones that get asked.

Will you abandon me, too? Will the day come when you won't want me either? How can I trust that you will always be there? What if I'm messy?

The cry for affirmation and security runs deep in the fatherless. As I watched him soak in my answer, I thought back to that early Morning Prayer experience I had more than two decades before. For no obvious reason, I had cried so hard that it turned into moaning, groaning, and unintelligible words. I grappled with understanding the intensity of this encounter with my Heavenly Father. I hadn't been in any particular frame of mind or experiencing anything unusual. This just seemed to happen. After what seemed like an extended period of time where my words were not understood, I spoke again clearly: "God, I want you to take me fishing. I want you to play ball with me."

I did not immediately reconcile that I was asking God to fulfill the broken promises of my father. They are the same exact words. Yet the first day I played ball with Jaden, and the day he caught his first fish, were nothing short of pure redemption!

Walking along with Jaden, in the quiet of my mind, I rehearsed the words that I would share with Jaden, when it was the right time...when he was old enough to understand these bigger concepts that were already so deeply affecting his heart.

"It's not the trips you might take abroad, Jaden, that concern me. It's the places you might go inside. You have to avoid the most dangerous countries, like Shame, Abandonment, and Unworthiness. Above all, you have to protect yourself from *Identity Theft*. Don't let anyone tell you who you are, because if you do, you might never find yourself. I spent years, in all my situations, hoping the Father would one day be with me and show me who I truly am...what my identity is. He spent those same years waiting for me to see that He is, and always has been, with me.

"Trust the whisper, Jaden. Pay attention to intuition. Nothing can separate you from His love, or mine! Whenever you feel disconnected or alone, it is just your Father saying, you are thinking, feeling, and believing fear-based lies. Trust Him! Know Him! He is your Abba. And He is with you wherever you go!"

How Did I Get Here?

How did I get here?
Well, let me say,
It was straightforward
In a roundabout way.

I went by the garden
And sampled almost every tree,
Eating rise and fall
Before I was free.

Both bitter and sweet I did taste,
Learning life lessons never to waste.
Inside my heart I found the plan,
Collected all the pieces to become a man.

With scars and ashes, I rose from the dead,
Solving the mystery running loose in my head.
Sometimes easy — sometimes hard,
Discovering from life — I am not barred.

Didn't know I was waiting for you, until you came.
Embracing just how much we are the same,
Spent time chasing the all-elusive,
Until I found love, the all-inclusive.

What I couldn't forgive caused me to leak like a sieve.
I plugged those darn holes, so I could live.
Now with my wholeness I offer to you
A better way for you to live true.

How did I get here?
Well, let me say,
It was straightforward
In a roundabout way.

Chapter 7

Papa, How Did You Get Here?

I made a surprise visit to see Jaden in San Francisco, arriving in time to go to his school with his mother to get him at the end of the day. I had envisioned sneaking into his classroom to catch him off-guard, but he was in the lobby and saw me right away through the glass doors.

He started jumping up and down yelling, "My papa's here! My papa's here!"

When I stepped inside, he came running and leaped into my arms. We hugged each other, holding on for dear life. Jaden asked, "Papa, how did you get here so fast?" I had spoken to him the night before from Los

Angeles, but he thought I was in Texas. I confessed my scheme to surprise him.

He wanted to show me to everyone. A teacher was passing by when Jaden reached out, tugged on her skirt and said with exuberance and eyes of delight, "This is my grandfather!" I knew exactly what he was saying: *Look, everybody, I have family. This is my papa and he loves me!*

As we were walking out of his school, Jaden asked me if I was here "just for today." I said, "Oh no, I'm going to spend a few days with you."

"Oh good. Because I've been missing you; and if you were only going to be here for today, that wouldn't work. But if you are going to be here for a few days, I know I'm going to be alright."

It was all I could do to keep from collapsing right then and there.

Maybe nobody else hears his cry quite the same way I do.

I hear you, sweet buddy. I see you. I understand you. I feel you. I know you. I get it. I get your fatherlessness. You have a hole, a big hole, inside your tender little heart. I will do everything I can to minimize your hollow place. The dysfunction in others, no matter how significant, is not your responsibility.

As I reached for his hand, I considered his question: "Papa, how did you get here so fast?" and immediately understood that this is perhaps the ultimate question of my life. *How did I get here?*

It was the question that I was asking myself as I felt the inspiration to write a book to my grandson, and to help others who are facing the wounds of fatherlessness. I had found something. I had finally gotten somewhere — where the pain of fatherlessness didn't ache as intensely as it had my entire life.

The answer is bigger than Jaden or me.

I Am Wanted.

Mom

I was sitting next to my mother, holding her hand. We had come to the final hours of her life. For the past five years, it had been my privilege to take care of my mom.

Forgiving my mother years before had afforded me the opportunity to be a good son to her. I have no regrets with my mom. I love her very much. I never missed the chance to honor her on Mother's Day, her birthdays, or Christmas, even during the times our relationship was stressed. And I found ways to bless her for no special reason. I would miss being able to love her and I would miss the love of my mother.

Through the most unusual circumstances, I had been alone with Mom for her final days. Tina went to get Jaden, in California, to surprise Mom for her birthday. She and Jaden shared a special bond. On the day Tina left, Mom took a turn for the worse, and sadly, they wouldn't make it in time. My niece, Kimi, was driving from Rhode Island but wouldn't make it in time either. My brother and sister wouldn't come. My cousin, Bridgett, and her husband came by to show love and support, as she had lost her mom (my Aunt Jo) only five weeks before.

Mom hadn't spoken or eaten in more than three days, and we were keeping her comfortable with pain meds. I'd been told that she could still hear me, so I kept talking to her. I had gone down memory lane several times as I sat beside her. I am most thankful for the conversations we had when I was able to ask her some difficult questions. Mom had bitterness toward her mother that she harbored even after her mother's death. Her father having been killed when she was so young left a scar. The saddest thing for me was knowing that Mom never found her bliss. Her four marriages were indicative of her search. I'm certain that she wanted to be a good mother and build a wonderful home for us, but just wasn't able to get there. She finished her life much better than you might have expected, actually outgrowing much of her dysfunction, but not before her kids were affected. I think my mom did the best she could. And that's enough for me.

The story I had told myself, all those years, was wrong. My mom wanted me. She just had her own father hole to deal with.

For the last three years, her quality of life had been awful. It was hard to witness. Nearing ten o'clock at night on the fifth day of her decline, out of the quiet,

I was struck with the reality that I needed to say my final goodbye.

I stood up and leaned over her. I kissed her forehead and said, "I'm here, Mom, and I love you very much. I have tried to be a good son, and I hope I never let you down." I told her that she had suffered enough, and it was okay for her to go. The emotional release staggered me. I sat back down and took her hand in mine.

Mom is gone!

I Am Worthy.

Dad

My father lived in my mind for most of my life. I created hardship by recreating the abandonment. I reached a place where all I wanted was a conversation. I just wanted to know *why*. I have been to forty-four states and fourteen countries, and the first thing I did when I arrived in every single one of them was check the local phone book to see if he was listed. My kids found his death certificate online in 1994, which showed that he had passed away in 1982. I had been searching for more than a decade for a man that wasn't even alive. And I still live with the bitter taste of unanswered questions.

I don't know the first thing about my father's father. And since my mother's father died when she was a child, I was lost. I have struggled with knowing who I am because fathers are paramount to discovering our identity, instilling a sense of worthiness, and providing our first glimpse of God. When fathers are missing or present but unavailable or violating, our heart goes on searches and our character can suffer.

The hollowness I felt inside had a heartbeat and a pulse. I didn't talk about it all the time, and I wasn't conscious of it every second of the day; but every experience was filtered through fatherlessness. I wasn't illegitimate, as my parents were married, but I had no sense of home or belonging. The recurring family break-ups in my childhood established a revolving door mentality. *Things aren't meant to last,* I told myself. And so I would break things that I built with sweat and blood, just to get ahead of the inevitable. I made things fall apart, subconsciously.

Maybe my thinking came about because men didn't seem to stay around long. Maybe it was the domestic violence — my mom repeatedly beaten in front of us as kids. Anger management in our house meant you managed to escape the anger in one piece. When my mom's husband knocked me unconscious at fifteen, I left home and never lived with them again.

I deserve better, I told myself, but the looming feeling of unworthiness made it hard to obtain.

You should have been there, Dad. I should have felt your loving arms a million times. I should have heard your voice cheering me on. I should have known your approval. You should have played ball with me and taken me fishing, like you promised. I should have known you, and I should have been known by you. I am worthy of all that you never gave me!

The effects of my missing father are undeniable, and yet I see now how I increased the negative ramifications in my life by the story I told myself. I bore the blame for things I had no control over. And the story I wrote about my missing father is more damaging than my father not being there. Abandonment and rejection don't establish our value. Just because my father didn't love me or want me didn't mean I wasn't worthy of being loved and wanted.

What was behind his decisions? How broken was he? Just how empty was his own soul? I know this; he will never know how much I wanted him or the love I held for him for so many years.

I forgive you, Dad. May you rest in peace.

Pastor

I'm aware of remarkable stepfathers and gifted mothers who step up and do wonders for kids without dads. Sometimes an extended family member, family friend, teacher, or a true mentor saves a kid from crashing and burning. But these situations are infrequent at best. Fatherlessness is pandemic.

For me, it was my childhood pastor, Frank Munsey, that stood in the gap. I lost contact with him for many years, but we reconnected after I was married and had children. He treated me like a son and provided a father-figure for me to love. Our relationship did not clear out all the debris in my reality, but his love was sustaining. He was a father in the truest sense, only wanting the best for me. Knowing he loved me kept me searching for answers. He was so many things to so many people; but for me, he will always be the greatest man I ever knew.

For fifty years, his hand, his hug, and his heart kept me going.

We lost him a few years ago, and I don't have the words to describe how much I miss him.

I Am Messy.

Faith

My original faith has always been messy. It taught that nothing can separate us from the love of God — that He would never leave us or forsake us — and yet, we had to continuously work to be *right* with God. It puts so much emphasis on giving, it makes receiving seem like sin. "There is no condemnation to them which are in Christ," yet shame is used to manipulate people into obedience to things that have no scriptural commandment. It reduced salvation to such fragile standards that trivial choices like clothing and hairstyles had to be institutionally approved. Hell, fire, and brimstone preaching created such fear that it contradicted "perfect love, which casts out all fear." It actually creates division so intense that being one with God, which is a primary purpose of Christianity, becomes an impossibility. Loving one's neighbor is excused so that derogatory labels can be acceptably applied to all those who are outside of our comfort zone.

As a man and a minister, I struggled with these concepts and grappled with the gross abuse and manipulation that had become obvious in my religious organization. It wasn't until my pastor friend betrayed me that the veil began to lift from my eyes.

Over time, I have realized this isn't isolated. It's widespread. While there are many churches that provide true safe havens and a culture of love, patience, and Godly instruction, mine was not one of them. But here's the thing: Most of us get caught up in looking at an organization and being angry with how the leaders behave, when the truth is there has to be a certain dysfunction inside of us to be compatible with any abuse that is embedded in the organizations where we seek emotional safety and relief. In my case, the dysfunction was fatherlessness, and I found it wherever I went.

I once thought this man, my friend, was brilliant. I thought he held my answer. I thought he was Dad. Yet what he did is not the work of a loving father. If I had listened to that still small voice, I would have been long gone, which would have prevented it from happening. In the end, he provided a great service and I'm thankful. He helped me discover The Father, although I'm sure it was unintended.

Religion can fail. Mine did. Faith never has to.

I was always too messy for my religion. I was too poor as a kid. I couldn't pay to play. I was too troubled.

When the church labeled me too messy to be included, I was being molested by older boys and girls. I lived in fear in my home, when I had one. When they thought I should have had it all figured out, I was still seeking answers. I looked for affirmation, identity, and worthiness but I failed to find it. Of course, looking back, I can see now that many others were living with Father Holes too. Many of them were dealing with real father hunger, not knowing the full height and depth of our Heavenly Father's love for them.

My faith has been my dance, sparring partner, and facilitator. It has been the missing pieces I tripped over, lying directly in my path. It has broken through the camouflage of personality, structure, and misrepresentation. It has laid glistening in the darkness and redeeming in the light. It has befriended me in isolation and comforted me in the crowds. It has revealed my rubbish and cleared away my debris. It has gone silent in confusion and spoken when I could hear. It has been undetectable, yet ever present. It has stripped me naked and clothed me with a single swoop. It has busted my legs and reset the bones. It has hid and revealed its position. It has charged me what I could not pay and paid my bill in full. It has declined to tolerate me, but refused to leave me alone. It has changed my failing concepts to a passing identity. It has created my hunger and made me full. It has ended my life and caused me to live. It has taken everything I had and given me everything I didn't. It has denied me access and granted me entry. It has led me to the end of limitless. It has taken away my labels and given me my name.

My faith is the invisible framework that holds me steady. It is the secret to my destiny. It is my faith that settles the past, proclaims the present, and points to the future. It is my faith that moves me into the impossible without fear of failure or success. It's my faith that reminds me that I have no right to quit. It is my faith that requires, with irrevocable demand, that I grant my Father access to all of me.

We are never too messy for God.

I Am Somebody's Son.

It's been forty years since my grandmother passed away. I can still see her smile. I can still hear her say, "There's my boy." She left me a feeling that I have drawn on many times. Long after she was gone, I had a remote sense of belonging to someone. It didn't fill the void of abandonment by my father, the conflicted emotions toward my mother, or the confusion with my faith, but it was something to cherish.

In some ways, her love was a two-edged sword. The fact that I had experienced her affection provided a means to believe in love itself. Yet, her no longer being there for ongoing support left me depleted and empty. In some ways, it intensified the absence of my father.

I tried over and over to acquire from others, the warmth and tenderness Grandma bestowed on me. Nobody could measure up. Nobody could do what she did. Eventually, my mother and I brought our relationship to a healthy place, and I benefitted from her love.

Yet in so many of my other important relationships, I manufactured pain, subconsciously, by attempting to turn the role of a mentor into that of a father. My father hunger was fierce. I ruined some valuable relationships, trying to be someone's boy, stressing them to produce what they were not designed to accomplish. The loss had the result of reinforcing feelings of abandonment and rejection, which then impacted my relationship with God.

Ultimately, I held God responsible for every human failure. I put my trust in men, and when they didn't deliver, I transferred blame to God. Which obscured my view of Him. My belief system conducted business with men as the voice of God and as His authority without the allowance for checks and balances. I was groomed to that end. I became a proponent of the culture. When I failed, I had nothing else to believe in.

Beyond my operational beliefs was an abiding notion that God was bigger than my context of Him could tolerate. Acting like you are God is quite different than recognizing who He is. Not until I was outside of the context I framed God in (where He had been framed for me) was I able to see Him as He is.

As He is, so are we, in this life. Separation only exists in perception.

After nearly three years away from ministry, and working on my personal life and marriage, the door opened for us to pastor again. Having already turned down another church, I was as careful as I could be to find confirmation that we should walk through that door. With peaceful hearts, we accepted the opportunity to pastor a church.

I had grown, persevering through my many life events. Transformational healing cleared much of my baggage. However, my deepest questions of worthiness and identity remained a quandary. I still couldn't get past "God can do anything but He doesn't seem to be doing what I need."

The occasion arose to merge our church with another one. There were many obvious benefits to joining our congregations. The strength of unity, the ability to accomplish more together than we could separately, and the opportunity to better care for the people. Yet, there are risks involved in everything.

Early success had most of us excited. I had less apprehension about expecting good things. And then wham! Our careful planning for every possible risk failed to detect an undercurrent. A leadership paradigm emerged that would be completely unacceptable. Abuse of authority, harsh and bitter treatment of people, and tremendous pressure for conformity was introduced. I was blindsided yet again. In the past, I would have taken matters into my own hands and probably made things worse. But this time, I knew I had to trust God to care for the people. My wife and I could not be a part of this ministry. We had merged with them, so I knew where the door was. I was out again!

It was my decision to leave, but we were forced to go without being allowed to say goodbye. I was enormously concerned for the people who had followed us there, and for the people already there. Our odd and quick departure should have been sufficient alarm, but for some, it wasn't. Many who stayed were terribly mishandled. I knew in my heart if people didn't see the problem for themselves, and leave on their own, no attempt to compel them would work. I was the best evidence of this truth.

Once more, I was tempted to go back into dark despair. Blaming myself for doing the wrong thing. Making the wrong decisions. Not being enough or good enough. Unworthy of divine providence. Just more lies to finally resolve. Eventually, I came to terms with all that had happened.

People fail. People prevent good things. We make our own trouble most of the time. What could have been, what was intended to be, would not happen. Sometimes we simply mismanage the divine things that come into our lives.

Our story continued to unfold. God's voice still gently and repetitiously worked with us. I was moving toward an understanding that my path would no longer be that of a pastor.

But God, what about that experience at ten years old, where the call to ministry seemed confirmed?

Holding on to that identity, rather than clarifying my life's work, had been a huge contributor to the calamity in my life. I was slowly letting the air out of my spacesuit, being retrofitted and granted the clarity I had longed for and was finally open to. Suddenly, I began to see a place for me that would define and clarify my calling.

Ministry goes far beyond church walls. One thing I learned in business is that you don't have to be at church to help people. And you don't have to only help people who attend or will attend your church. I learned through experience that helping people where they are is effective. The master plan will evolve.

I would continue to minister to people but from a different platform.

One last effort would be made that would verify divine intention. We got a call to "try out" for a church in another state that was seeking a pastor. With emerging clarity, I had just enough residual effects from my life-long identity to flirt with this some more.

There was a nagging feeling, from the first call, that this was not for us. But that pastor identity thing in me was hungry. It needed something to eat. We took our turn and it went well. I actually got excited and left thinking we would pastor there. After we returned home, my wife began to talk to me and took all the wind out of my sails. (These dog gone women and their reality-based intuition. Dang it.)

There were very obvious elements of the religious things I hated. The potential for power struggles, harsh bitter judgments, and doctrines of men were clearly visible.

"But wait a minute. Aren't we prepared for this type of challenge? Hasn't everything we've been through made us qualified for this kind of situation?" I coaxed.

"Well, you and God can work it out then," my wife said. "I don't want anything to do with it." She went on to remind me that we had spent an extended period of time talking about the rest of our lives and this was not what we had decided we wanted to do.

I made the call and told the pastor, "I know I was positive when we were there with you. I expressed interest and commitment, but I need to withdraw from consideration. Even if you chose us, we would not be able to accept."

He said he would pass the information on to the board but wanted to leave our name in consideration. That touched my father hunger, again. *Maybe Tina will be the one to change her mind.* In my search for significance, I would need to further resolve what I am uniquely called to do. What seemed like rejection was actually a father's protection.

We moved to Indiana where we methodically reconstructed our lives. I worked another business, remodeled a house, planted tons of flowers, and started gardening. In fact, I was working in the garden when Tina came out to share the information that would change our lives forever: Monica was pregnant, and the father would not be in the picture.

She came from California to live with us. We would go through this as a family. After I dealt with the initial heartbreak, I knew it was important to get ready to celebrate the birth of this baby.

I Am Unique.

When I was able to release my childhood and pastor identities, life took on new meaning. My desire to help other people has become stronger than ever. Mostly because I'm no longer attempting to fulfill my purpose within a context of restriction. I don't limit myself to professional ministry.

I have discovered that what makes us upset and what makes us the most satisfied are indicators of destiny. Not a full explanation but more of a direction. Significance will always be found in the contributions we make to advance others and in the problems we solve. The weight of self-indulgence, at some point, becomes too heavy to carry.

The plight of the fatherless is a worldwide crisis and I'm moved to respond. My future exploits will be to help people connect the dots to obtain affirmation, a sense of worthiness, and secure their identity. We are not our titles; we are our connections.

It may not be possible, for many reasons, to connect to our fathers. But, it is always possible to connect to our Heavenly Father. Observing my own life and being a student of other people's pain has alerted me to the cry for Father within masses of people. Guy Corneau, author of, *Absent Fathers, Lost Sons, The Search for Masculine Identity,* makes the most remarkable statement: "regaining the essential 'second birth' into manhood lies in gaining the ability to be *a father to ourselves.*"

I would further express that true spirituality (maturity) flows from allowing God to be to you what He already is to Himself. He lacks nothing and makes everything He has available to us. When we make the connection, our lives change. Our only defeat is giving up.

Now that I can see God for who He is, I am at peace with who I am, and I'm not driven to perform to someone else's standard or live a life designed or expected by someone else. I am free to embrace my own uniqueness.

I have become the father I never had and the father I never was. My unique qualifications position me to bring healing and hope to those suffering with fatherlessness.

My Father Is With Me.

I have come to know that the human experience is both a gift and a mystery that needs to be solved. Nobody has ever done me wrong, directly. What was done was done to themselves first. And because of proximity, I might have been scorched. Likewise, the error of my ways only reflected an improper valuation of my own life. And by association, other people were affected by my actions. I am responsible for the pain I *accept* and the pain I *cause*. It's a mark of nobility to minimize both.

The things that happened to me weren't as bad as the stories I told myself about those things. I kept close the very things I wanted to go away. It wasn't until I divided external experiences from internal worthiness that I was able to understand *the perfect in chaos.*

With the shattered pieces of my life experiences and the turmoil of my self-inflicted wounds, I needed a miracle.

The repetitive lyrical phrases that continuously pounded against my soul were only lies, borrowed from human defect, and plagiarized as my own.

I peeled back traditional instruction until all that was left is divine intention. God is not in a state of anger. He's not ambitious to belittle, shame, or bring judgment. In fact, His desire is relentless to bring about well-being and abundance. God is a covering, a protector, and a supplier. He meets needs and fulfills dreams. He is Father! And, He wants only the best for us.

Test gravity and see if you don't fall. Stick your hand into a flame and see if you don't get burned. These are principles we discover, useful for the endeavors of mankind. But they are not retributions from a psychopath. The Father is not into spiritual child abuse, domestic violence, or forced marriage. He simply will not beat us into submission. We suffer consequences when we violate principles put in place to keep us safe. God is not saying, "That's what you get."

He takes no pleasure in our pain and the feelings of separation we experience.

Broken, shattered, and fragmented, I didn't even know where all the pieces of *me* were. My brokenness attracted broken people and dysfunctional religiosity. Theological rhetoric and legalistic doctrines of men only intensified my dilemma. I was reared, mentored, and became a propagator of the ugly side of Christianity. I was taught to hate, shaped in fear, and trained in manipulation. I was in the hands of men who failed me. And I, most assuredly, disappointed others.

I was bitter before I knew what it was. Disillusioned with no other lighthouse in sight. Twisted into misalignment with reality. Standing on ground that wouldn't stop moving. Wanting out, but too afraid to leave. I had to fail, violate my own innocence, to awaken.

What I hated in others was firmly rooted in me. Forgiving myself made forgiving others a walk in the park. I discovered a life in forgiveness that the lack of forgiveness kept hidden. I found in the Father an endless love, limitless grace, and my identity.

Finding my father was the purest desire of my life. To understand that He was there from the beginning, present for every heartache, celebration, moment of darkness, and point of light changed me. My feelings and thoughts of separation were flawed perceptions. He was the One on the outside looking in.

I have never been without my Father!

How did I get here, Jaden?
Well, let me tell you.

I often dreamed of a more pleasant introduction to the world. I had inherent value. I was prepackaged with purpose. I was preloaded with the necessary gifts to fulfill my destiny. But my parents and caregivers were simply not prepared for the responsibility of shaping my wings, wisdom, and wonder.

Standing in the delivery room, holding you, Jaden, peering into your eyes and reaching for your soul, I poured myself into you. As I was giving you everything I had, making sure you received the proper introduction to the life you deserve, for the first time in my life, I knew exactly how God feels about me. As my entire life played on the screen of my mind, I understood unconditional love. I had spent my life searching for my missing father and it made me miss the Father that was always there. My heavenly Father held me, as I held you. As I spoke into you, He spoke into me.

The doctor thought you were just another ordinary birth. The world thought you were just another father-less child. Not a chance. I see you. I feel you. I understand you, and I vow to do my part, to show you that you are loved, wanted, and worthy.

Thank you, God! Thank you! Thank you! Thank you! I wrote this book for you, Jaden (and for all who suffer with fatherlessness). I will not keep any good thing from you. It's good that you know my story, warts and all, so you can see I cleared a path for you to live an abundant life. And you will always have this book to remember the courage I found to help breathe life into you. When my time comes and I'm no longer with you, Jaden, the Father will be!

I've tried to prevent as much of your pain as I can. You will have to personally finish finding your freedom from fatherlessness.

Always remember this, Jaden: The greatest act of love I have ever seen and experienced is the healing of the fatherlessness in me.

I will spend the rest of my days demonstrating to you, that you are worthy of the best life has to offer. I love you, Jaden, my papa boy!

Epilogue

A Father's Heart!

"Rick, we are second cousins."

His words set off a chemical reaction I was extremely familiar with — it's the metabolic reaction of 'hope for answers.'

I was just finishing the last chapter of this book, and of course I wondered about the timing.

Could it be? That just as I am writing the last part of my story, I will finally have the answers I've been searching for? That I will finally know what happened to my dad — why he left me? That I will finally be connected to the family I'd never been able to meet?

Having lived decades searching for my dad and knowledge about his side of the family, I was stunned when I was contacted by a family member who had worked extensively on the Amitin family tree. In a matter of minutes, I had more information than I'd ever had after years of searching and reaching out to possible family members. I now knew the names of my great-grandfather and all the relatives connected up to him. When I saw the picture of my great-grandfather, all I could do was stare into the photograph, and let the tears flow.

The excitement overwhelmed me. As I carefully studied the few pictures and names of the family I never knew, I sat with surreal emotions swirling all around me, engulfed in imagination, and devouring every morsel.

"This means so much to me." I paused to find adequate words. "In fact, I'm finishing a book about my life journey without a dad. Thank you so much for providing this life-changing genealogical history."

He promised to put me in contact with many other family members and told me how excited many of them would be to discover me. A few days later, I received an email that closed with, "Welcome to the bosom of your paternal family, Rick."

My heart nearly exploded. For a man who searched, and longed for any kernel of family identity, this was a feast.

Since this email, my cousin seems to have disappeared. My last three emails, over several weeks, have not been answered.

At first, familiar lyrics and feelings showed their ugly head. *What is this? An Amitin thing? A few moments of deep connection and then complete abandonment... just like my dad?*

It didn't take more than a second for the pain of abandonment, rejection, confusion, and anger to resurface and stir things up. But after processing through these natural feelings of disappointment and frustration, I knew that this was a gift — evidence of the healing I've been working so hard for.

There is nothing here that belongs to me! I may never hear from him or any other family member again. And, I will be sad if that happens. But I will not buy back into the lies, and the feelings I have healed.

I mated, married, and became one with seeds of destruction, with devastating consequences. I lived lies that festered and continuously infected my life with disease (dis-ease). My experience of a maternal break, a paternal abandonment, and religious failure destined me to ruination.

Ah, but LOVE has other plans.

It most assuredly involved the unraveling of my mental, emotional, and spiritual knot. Even my physical well-being was woven into the mix. There remained, through all of my confusion, the tiniest belief that an answer existed. That small lifeline eventually led me to an open heart and A Father's Heart too!

My father wound and the related elements birthed my sense of unworthiness, not being wanted, and the theft of my identity. The lyrics that played softly in the background, and loudly at opportunistic times, came to an end when I discovered my truth: I came from love, I am love, and I give love away. My mess came from brokenness that flowed from a breach in my relationship with love. It didn't begin with me but was established in me through bloodline, environment, and early traumatic events. I was not the author of the trauma that created this family dynamic in me. But I was a carrier. And, I acted out in ways that perpetuated these traits.

I thought I was unworthy, and I was around others prone to such declarations, and they were all too ready to reinforce the notion. When I heard the words, *"you are my son in whom I am well pleased,"* as I held Jaden and poured into him for the first time, it removed the lie and established my understanding of eternal worthiness. If your training causes you to think for God, it will be difficult for you to hear what He is saying. For so many years, I could only go so far and no further. I kept coming up short. When I comprehended divine intention for me, I found my place of belonging.

The capacity for darkness is the capacity for Light. Desire for love, affirmation, worthiness, and identity cannot sit idle. It continuously moves toward barrenness or fulfillment. It drives pain or it drives joy. It's never too late to change direction. What we believe is a default setting *can* be replaced by being deliberate. Nothing is more detrimental than to ignore divine intention. The Father wanted me, and still does. The Father wants you too.

And there is the work that we fatherless must do.

I went to a writer's retreat in the early stages of writing this book. I prepared before I arrived for the three-day workshop by bringing my emotions and thoughts together in anticipation. I didn't know what to expect, only that I was to attend. The first day, we were given the exercise of painting pictures of our lives' defining moments on a sheet of paper.

I looked at the blank piece of paper, and before I could pick up the paintbrush, I was overcome with grief. I didn't want to look at my life. Horror coursed through my veins. I had to leave the table and go outside to talk to the Father. Maybe I should have been concerned about what the others might think, but I wasn't. The presence of God was so real to me in that moment. What I heard was, *"That's not you, Rick. That's darkness. You are Light. The darkness will not prevent the Light from breaking through."*

I collected myself and rejoined the group. I don't even remember what I painted. I returned home, still interacting with the experience. Wanting the words of love to be true. Hoping I could hang on to them.

After a few days of meditating and processing this defining moment in the making, I found some clarity.

Sitting alone in my home office, I took out a piece of paper and drew a line down the middle of the page. On the left side, I would write what I thought of me; and on the right, I would write what God thought of me. I began to list what I thought of myself. I had to get another sheet of paper. I didn't think very highly of me. I didn't like me very much. I filled the left side with an awful and hateful critique, giving myself what I thought I deserved. I got so upset that I just wanted to stop writing, but I continued until I had nothing left to put down.

When I moved to the right side, I couldn't write anything. I was paralyzed. I just sat there, scared that God thinks the same things about me.

Slowly my anger at myself dissipated and a wonderful feeling emerged. I felt impressed to write, *"I Love You!"*

My hand was shaking and my heart was beating fast. Through the biggest tear drops I had ever seen, I managed to get the words written down and then was urged to keep going, *"I want you. You are worthy. You are unique. I've been there for every moment of your life. I was with you in your darkness. I will never leave you. You are my son in whom I am well pleased!"*

I was tempted to argue my disbelief but couldn't. For the better part of an hour, I received a love-letter that was literally out of this world.

I have a Dad and He loves me.

Human worthiness is based on human judgment — deciding what each other should get. It often involves people taking life energy from one another, creating a war mentality resulting in greater separation and division. We can judge behavior but not motivation (the heart). Empathy and kindness is what we are best suited for. Here is our only guarantee: love never fails.

It's crucial that we understand that authentic worthiness is what we are born with. And it comes with an R.S.V.P. Accept it and the world will open up to you. Live it out and you will discover your place in the vast sea of life. Act on it and your unique gifts unfold. Significance evolves from your story. Your pain folds into your purpose. A sense of worthiness makes all things possible. You'll live with an open heart because the Father's heart will be in you.

An honest reflection will surely reveal that there was always someone that loved you, wanted you, and cared for you. Even if you couldn't receive it.

Some believe your life changes when you find God, but I believe God is everywhere in everything. He's neither lost nor hiding. It's not about us going to God. He is forever attempting to come to us. He has been working on our behalf our whole life. He has loving arms trying to hold you. Let Him do it.

He will pull divine circumstances, situations, and people into your life if you will give up the fast food and quick fixes. Artificial and synthetic living leaves us cold, undone, and disconnected. Speak truth to the lies, knowing that your identity isn't in all the mess that we and others create. Your identity is in what you do with all of you.

I have hope for the fatherless. And I have hope for you!

About Rick

Rick Amitin is an Inspirational Author and Speaker, whose mission is to provide a compassionate solution to the pandemic of fatherlessness. Abandoned by his father as a small child, Rick grappled with a lack of identity and sense of worthiness, as well as the nightmarish consequences of living from the pain of his abandonment, for more than fifty years. As an Ordained Minister with a conservative Pentecostal organization, Rick preached the love of God, but it wasn't until he became a grandfather that the Purest Father's Love catalyzed his own journey of deep healing and complete life transformation.

Rick is a Certified Behavioral Analyst from The Institute for Motivational Living, a Licensed Insurance Agent who built a multi-million-dollar insurance business, and a Transformational Life Coach. He is a lifelong student with a number of certifications, has attended numerous seminars in personal development, and is an avid reader and researcher. Rick has received training by some of the leading voices of our time: Ford Taylor, Jack Canfield, Sanford G. Kulkin, and Kevin Knebl. Rick is a former member of The Writers Guild of Texas and The Dallas Fort Worth Writers Workshop, and served on the Dallas Fort Worth Writers Conference Committee.

Rick's raw-polish approach to sharing his story, mixed with his deliciously wholesome sense of humor and his hard-earned wisdom and skills, delivers life-changing experiences for his readers, students, and audiences. Compassionate for the plight of the fatherless, yet insistent about personal responsibility, Rick will make you laugh, cry, and gasp as you walk with him into a life of deep satisfaction and fulfillment.

Rick is creating online courses to accompany his retreats, seminars, and speaking engagements. He resides in San Francisco, CA with his wife, Tina, of thirty-four years. He loves the ocean, a good book, and always keeps a pen and paper handy. He is a father, grandfather, and great-grandfather.

My Special Invitation

You've read the book...

What should you do next?

As you know, intense pain, roots of dysfunction, anger, and feelings of disconnection aren't simply wished away. What you may not know is that everything you need to heal is already inside of you, underneath the layers, and multilayers, of pain and longing.

It is necessary to identify violations and self-inflicted wounds, and we also need a strategy and path forward. My own experience taught me that deliberate actions and expert support are critical to work through all of this and create the life you crave.

If you are committed to healing the roots of dysfunction and disconnection, and create the life you desire, I invite you to head over to **www.IfOnlyIHadADad.com**, download the workbook I developed to go alongside this book, and then stay connected to this growing community, which is committed to ending the pandemic of Fatherlessness.

**Get started by downloading
your workbook today!**

www.IfOnlyIHadADad.com

Made in United States
North Haven, CT
10 June 2022

20082845R00102